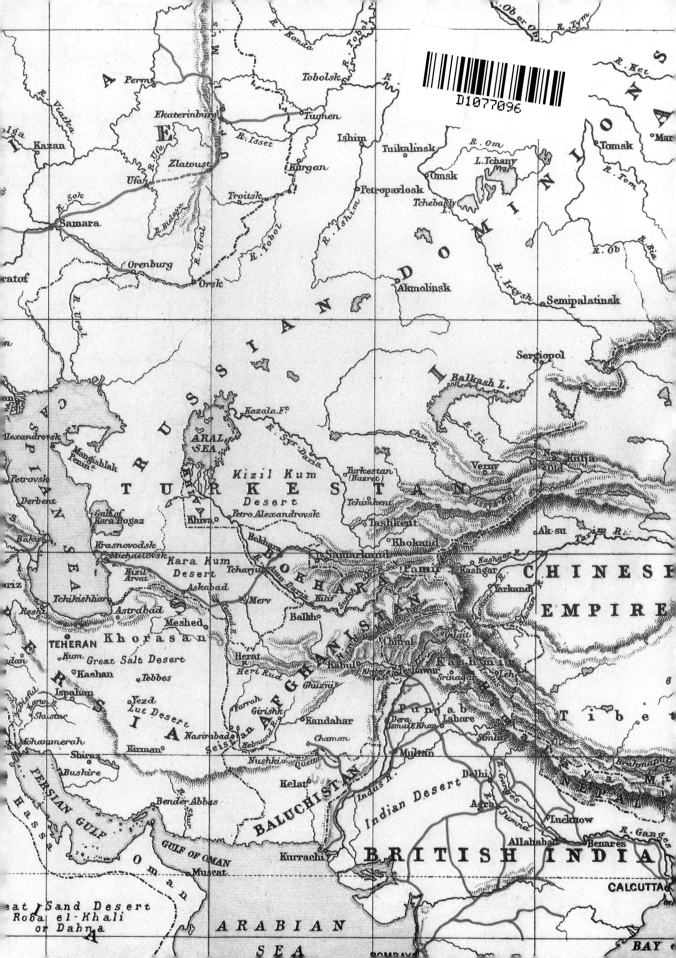

TRAVELS
WITH A
SUPERIOR
PERSON

TRAVELS WITH A SUPERIOR PERSON

BY THE
MARQUESS CURZON OF KEDLESTON
GOLD MEDALLIST (1895) AND PRESIDENT (1911-1914)
OF THE ROYAL GEOGRAPHICAL SOCIETY

EDITED BY
PETER KING
INTRODUCED BY
ELIZABETH LONGFORD

Beyond the East, the sunrise, beyond the West, the sea,
And East and West, the wander-thirst that will not let me
be.
GERALD GOULD

SIDGWICK & JACKSON
LONDON

First published in Great Britain in 1985
by Sidgwick & Jackson Limited
1 Tavistock Chambers, Bloomsbury Way
London WC1A 2SG

Designed and produced by
Shuckburgh Reynolds Limited
289 Westbourne Grove, London W11 2QA

Design copyright © Shuckburgh Reynolds Limited

ISBN 0 283 99716 8

Designed by Behram Kapadia
Picture research by Peter King

Typesetting by SX Composing Ltd, Rayleigh, Essex
Printed and bound by Purnell & Sons Limited, Bristol

FRONTISPIECE: *The Honourable George Curzon painted by Spy
(Vanity Fair, 1885)*

Contents

Illustrations

ILLUSTRATIONS

Pictures on pp. 12, 21, 22, 23, 47, 64, 84, 93, 162
by kind permission of the Royal Geographical
Society
Pictures on pp. 29, 41, 49, 54, 79, 107 from Mary
Evans Picture Library

Introduction

Elizabeth Longford

To be called "superior" today would not be the highest of compliments – unless of course one were a nun or a brand of tea. Yet the young George Curzon was not only given this soubriquet when up at Oxford as a scholar of Balliol College – "My name is George Nathaniel Curzon/I am a most superior person" – but he himself recorded it with pride when a rising politician of thirty-two. In 1891 he was elected a member of the Crabbet Club, a literary and mildly athletic coterie, many of them "Souls", hosted by Curzon's cousin by marriage, Wilfrid Scawen Blunt. It was customary for members at these esoteric gatherings to compete both in poetry and tennis. That year Oscar Wilde chose for the subject of the verse competition: "In Praise of Myself". Curzon's amusing offering began with the couplet: "Charms and a man I sing, to wit – a most superior person/Myself, who bears the fitting name of George Nathaniel Curzon...."

The name was "fitting" because the Curzons dated from the Norman Conquest. The three names recited together had a superbly dignified ring and Curzon included a dignified carriage and countenance among the signs of his "superiority". Admittedly the dignity sometimes seemed to deteriorate into stiff-necked arrogance – but this was partly because of severe curvature of the spine which necessitated his encasing himself in an unbending steel corset.

Intellectual brilliance was also part of his undoubted "superiority". He had won all the prizes at Eton and again at Oxford, and was a Fellow of that prestigious graduate college, All Souls. His only academic failure had been to get a Second in Greats (the Oxford degree in classical history and philosophy) instead of the expected First. This humiliation bit deep and provoked Curzon into his famous vow: "Now I shall devote the rest of my life to showing the examiners that they have made a mistake." One might say that this vastly entertaining and erudite book of collected travel tales is one of the many ways in which Curzon did indeed prove his examiners wrong.

His presence and dignity were so prodigious that someone said of him, "George Curzon is the only man I know who could make a speech in his pyjamas without looking ridiculous." On the other hand there were times when he did not at all mind looking ridiculous and even chose to do so. After the Crabbet Club dinners the members would sally out into the Sussex dawn, swim naked in the lake and play tennis naked on the lawn. The young George loved dressing up for charades as much as the older George would love the dressing up entailed in being Viceroy of India. That he did not always want to look like a viceroy or as if he were mounted on the summit of an elephant, will appear convincingly from the pages that follow.

Nor do I entirely believe in his arrant snobbery as related by his first biographer, Lord Ronaldshay. The celebrated story goes that Curzon saw soldiers bathing in some public place when he suddenly exclaimed, "Dear me! I had no idea the lower classes had such white skins." Curzon had seen more skins of brown, black and yellow hue than any of his aristocratic contemporaries and he knew all about that sort of thing. Of course it may have been one of his jokes against himself.

Nevertheless one must confess that it was a vein of pomp and magnificence in his character which responded so vividly to the glowing Orient. As we shall see, Memnon, the Colossus of Thebes, towering against an Egyptian sky, was also a "superior person" in his own way. To describe the resplendent dyes of the carpets in Bokhara was sheer pleasure, appealing to his taste and style. His writing is rich in purple patches; but what colour could be more appropriate to the "gorgeous East"?

Not that these fascinating tales are all descriptive. Two at least are examples of Curzon's gift for research and detective work: "The Billiard Table of Napoleon" and "The Voice of Memnon". I found the latter especially intriguing, having seen another colossus standing outside the Valley of the Kings at Luxor. But the only "voice" I heard coming from somewhere beneath the statue's monumental limbs was that of an Egyptian boy trying to sell me a tiny green object. It turned out to be a fake scarab such as Curzon mentions.

At last the boy gave up and, surprisingly, pushed the scarab into my hand. "Here, have it anyway."

On the whole, however, this volume is splendidly descriptive, its aim being to entertain, to make us *see*. Curzon divides travel books, his own in particular, into two kinds: the ones that simply make us see and are therefore beautiful and romantic; and the others that give information, which will perhaps be useful to the British Foreign Office. The first kind he refers to as *Tales* of travel, the second as *Problems* of the Far East or the Persian *Question*. But if this volume has more tales and fewer problems than the collection republished in 1984 (*A Viceroy's India*) the problems and questions can never be entirely eliminated, above all when Curzon enters Russia in Asia.

One is bound to compare what he wrote twenty or thirty years before the Russian Revolution with what we know of Russia some seventy years after it. For instance, in trying to get a travel permit from the Caucasus to Tiflis, he writes of "the tortuous windings of diplomatic policy or official intrigue at St. Petersburg". Change the last name, and you have jumped forward a hundred years.

It is difficult to choose one "purple passage" from among so many alluring examples. As a brief "purple", I would go for his exquisite description of the "Black Sand" in the desert of Kara Kum:

> Ever and anon a solitary sand-column, raised by a passing puff of air, starts up, and giddily revolving on its fragile axis whirls away over the plain. This spectacle extends to the northern horizon, where it is lost in the mirage which is prevalent in these parts, and the liquid tremulous medium of which transforms the featureless dismal plain into luscious lakes of water with floating islets of trees.

But indeed all Curzon's writing about deserts is full of almost mystical reflections and double visions, like nothing so much as one of the phantom oases themselves. I know of no modern writers who possess this refractional gift except Patrick Leigh Fermor and Laurens van der Post.

With his wide experience of the world's most seductive prospects, Curzon is a master of the learned yet taut comparison, say, of Saracenic austerity at Samarkand with the additional Florentine intricacy at Delhi. The Taj Mahal he describes as "that most perfect of tributes to a lost love" where "the luxuriant elegance of Florentine details is wedded to the august symmetry of Saracenic forms", whose true style "is expressed in grandeur rather than delicacy". Curzon possesses the catholicity of taste that a good traveller needs. Perhaps he is a little sentimental about the tomb in the Taj. Mumtaz, the Shah's "lost love", was a formidable woman who had her enemies squashed to death under the feet of elephants. I imagine her more like Irma the Nazi than an Eastern beauty with the eyes of a gazelle. However, the British, when writing about the East, have to be allowed a little latitude in the way of sentiment: they usually make good use of it, as did the authors of the *Omar Khayyam* and *Hassan*; likewise of these *Travels*.

For longer and more elaborate purple passages I would go to Curzon's "Waters of Babylon", and Tamerlane's Tomb.

The "Superior Person" was not a religious man but, like many such, he had a strong sense of *lacrimae rerum* or "the tears of things". This comes out in his moving reflections on change and decay in central Asia.

> The traveller feels like a wanderer at night in some desecrated graveyard, amid crumbling tombstones and half-obliterated mounds. A cemetery, not of hundreds of years but of thousands, not of families or tribes but of nations and empires, lies outspread around him; and . . . in falling tower or shattered arch, he stumbles upon some poor unearthed skeleton of the past.

Curzon was an incurable name-dropper – but only of the most superior kind. Alexander the Great (with an amusing modern anecdote attached), Napoleon, Dr Johnson, Matthew Arnold and many classical stars all feature, adding interest as well as a cachet to his *Travels*. He can also be a journalist with the best of them. In his "Notes from the Nile", published in *The World* (1883), he demonstrates a sharp eye for Western tourists in Egypt, especially the "American ladies doing the round of Europe (it is hard to believe that Egypt is not a part of Europe) in neatly-fitting ulsters and curly straw hats ..." Curzon was to marry a beautiful American heiress, Mary Leiter. But it is to his far more polished sketches of Eastern ladies found in these *Travels* that one turns for his most striking effects. For example, the ladies of Bokhara:

> Not only were the features concealed behind a heavy black horse-hair veil, falling from the top of the head to the bosom, but their figures were loosely wrapped up in big blue cotton dressing gowns [instead of those neatly-fitting ulsters!], the sleeves of which are not used but are pinned together over the shoulders at the back and hang down to the ground, where from under this shapeless mass of drapery appear a pair of feet encased in big leather boots. After this I should be more or less than human if I were to speak enthusiastically of the Bokhara ladies.

This short passage is a good example of Curzon's agreeable wit. It becomes even more human in his account of striking a bargain with a Tartar:

> He likes to be patted on the back and whispered to in the ear; and if, after a prolonged struggle, repeated perhaps for two or three days, you can at length get hold of his hand and give it a hearty shake, the bargain is clinched and the purchase is yours.

His wit can change at will into black humour, as when the unfortunate dancing girl of Keneh drowns, or into broad humour when the "courtly Seyid" at Nejev (Curzon's spelling) is run away with by the fiery Arab steed he tries in vain to lend to the cautious Curzon, who safely continued his "travels with a donkey" instead. Or there is the extremely funny account of the young Curzon borrowing (without permission) a top-hat in which to present himself to the Shah at Teheran.

That Curzon took his travel books, whether of the instructive or entertaining variety, extremely seriously, is proved by the postponement of his (blissfully happy) marriage for over four years – until his world travels were completed. He wrote after his wife's death:

> I told her that while I felt from the beginning that we were destined for each other, I had not dared to speak, and had even run the risk of losing her because there was certain work in my scheme of Asiatic travel which I had resolved to do, and which I could not ask any married woman to allow her husband to carry out.

This curious mixture of cold calculation and sensitive consideration was characteristic of Curzon.

His arduous journeys on horseback meant that he was in some degree of pain most of the time; indeed he had to convalesce in the south of France or Switzerland after many of his expeditions. "Intrepid traveller" is a cliché that is given new vitality by Curzon's exploits.

Does his own definition of a "great man" apply to him personally? He cites "stability, principle and faith" as the combined ingredients of true greatness, an interesting trio. Curzon himself lacked stability. Highly-strung and emotional, he sobbed when he heard that he had missed the premiership. He was a round-the-world traveller, notwithstanding, who was great in his courage, endurance and amazing stocks of knowledge. It is a matter for rejoicing that the modern reader can now follow this extraordinary man not only into India and Afghanistan, but also to Turkestan, Persia, Greece and Egypt, with witty glances into Japan and China as well.

Editor's Note

If Lord Curzon were alive today, he would approve of the booksellers putting only one of his books in their "Travel" sections and that would be *Tales of Travel*, published in 1923 shortly before his death. Yet he was one of the most prolific travel writers in the English language of the past one hundred years; and much of his political writing is shot through with perceptive description and advice for other travellers. The most famous example of the latter is the train journey I have included in this book, taken from *Russia in Central Asia* published in 1889.

When I compiled *A Viceroy's India* (1984) I selected some of Curzon's essays from *Tales of Travel* and some from the posthumous selection *Leaves from a Viceroy's Note-book* (1926), confining myself to material about India and that subcontinent. The present selection derives from Curzon's travels in other lands, and the pieces are selected from those two books and from *Russia in Central Asia*. Between 1882 and 1894 Curzon travelled a great deal, with brief interludes as a Fellow of All Souls, Lord Salisbury's private secretary and Member of Parliament for Southport. He carried small note-books (which may still be read in the library of the India Office), and from these he later both transcribed articles for the *Times* and other periodicals, and rewrote for his books. His later travels were extensive but not, I believe, as productive of great writing as these global travels when he was in his twenties and early thirties.

Very little editing on my part is therefore called for, and I have confined this to shortening the long essay, "The Voice of Memnon" and editing the four consecutive chapters from *Russia in Central Asia* that come at the end of this book to exclude the quite detailed railway and demographic information which Curzon probably intended to be put to good use by military intelligence departments, when they came to plan campaigns which he was certain would be undertaken in his lifetime, a view shared by several of his contemporaries including Kitchener. My selection from Curzon's account of his travels on the Transcaspian railway ends then at the point where his overt political comments begin.

Curzon chose the illustrations for all his books himself, and in addition built up a vast and invaluable collection of photographs, now deposited in the India Office Library and worth its weight in gold. Despite the fact that the charges rendered by the British Library for the privilege of photographing this material are considerably more than its weight in gold, I have thought it right to supplement his own choice of pictures with further photographs from this collection. In a very few cases, noted in the list of illustrations, pictures have been obtained from other sources.

I am particularly grateful to Lady Alexandra Metcalfe, Lord Curzon's daughter, for her help and encouragement, and to Lord Scarsdale and the Trustees of the Kedleston Estate for their assistance. Dr John Hemming, Director of the Royal Geographical Society, and his staff have been most generous in their support, as have been the Director and staff of the India Office. My thanks are also due to Mr William Husselby for providing facilities for my work and to Mrs Cherry Carroll for her generous encouragement. Mrs Jennifer Wates kindly translated the classical texts, as she did for *A Viceroy's India*, and Mr Toby King translated the antique Spanish. Mr Roy MacLaren is due special thanks for asking for "more" after he had read *A Viceroy's India*.

In conclusion I must thank Lord Curzon, wherever he may be, for the pleasure I have gained from editing his work, for his unfailing good humour which makes it a pleasure and not a duty to reread and read again his timeless words, and for setting a standard of style that I can admire if I cannot emulate.

PETER KING
London 1985

Introduction to Tales of Travel

Forsan et haec olim meminisse iuvabit.

Virgil., *Aeneid* i. 203.

Perchance some day will there be pleasure
in remembering even these things.

I WONDER if it may be permitted to a politician to remember the days when he was only secondarily a politician, and when he found a chief zest of life in travel, not indeed in aimless and desultory travel, but in travel with that most generally unpopular of all attributes, a purpose. In my case the purpose was twofold: to see the beautiful and romantic and, above all, the ancient things of the earth – a taste which I probably share with most travellers, but which took me preferably to distant Oriental lands; and, secondly, to see how far the study of those places and peoples would help me to form an opinion on the Eastern responsibilities and destinies of Great Britain. This was a subject in which I took from boyhood an absorbing interest, and which led me to devote many months in each year, and, after I had entered Parliament, the bulk of my Parliamentary holidays, to wanderings in all parts of Asia from the Mediterranean to the China Seas. The results of these studies were embodied long ago in books of a more or less serious character, and I have no intention to repeat any part of that story here.

But in the course of these journeys I visited many other countries and places, twice going round the world, and exploring unfrequented spots, not in Asia only, but in Europe, Africa, and America. In certain of these cases I studied rather deeply some subjects of more than ephemeral interest. I came across some remarkable persons, and I made notes of many curious scenes. I have found it a diversion, in the turmoil of public life, to put these notes into final shape, and have even thought that they might prove of interest to a larger audience.

After I had spent some years in travelling and in writing about my travels, it gave me greater pleasure to be awarded the Gold Medal of the Royal Geographical Society for exploration and research than it did to become a Minister of the Crown; and every moment that I could snatch from politics – before they finally captured and tied me down – I devoted to the pursuit of my old love.

Even now, if in rare moments I seek literary distraction, it is in the perusal of works of travel and exploration that I am certain to find it; and when foreign affairs are specially vexatious or perplexing, recreation and repose come stealing in upon me from the memories of the past. I am once again in the wilds of Asia, or on the mountain-tops, or amid the majestic monuments of bygone ages. At one moment the wonders of nature fill the picture, at another, the scarcely less remarkable masterpieces of man. The shut pages of the past unroll, and the characters written upon them a quarter of a century and more ago start again to life. On these occasions I remember, almost with a start, that it is the

It gave me greater pleasure to be awarded the Gold Medal of the Royal Geographical Society for exploration and research than it did to become a Minister of the Crown.

I am again the youthful rover.

12

middle-aged and sedentary politician who in the early nineties shot Ovis Poli on the Pamirs, who nearly foundered in a typhoon off the coast of Annam, and was reported as murdered in Afghanistan. I am again the youthful rover who was stoned by furious Spaniards on the quays of Valencia; who climbed to the crater of Etna in deep snow by night to witness the glory of the sunrise over Sicily and the Straits; who saw the cone of Adam's Peak throw its shadow, also at sunrise, over the folded mist wreaths that smoked above the steaming valleys of Ceylon; who stayed with Amir Abdur Rahman Khan at Kabul, and with the afterwards murdered Mehtar of Chitral; who arrested the Abbot of a Korean monastery for stealing his watch and purse, and was himself arrested as a spy in Khorasan and in Wakhan; who was wrecked off the coast of Dalmatia, and explored the source of the Oxus; who wrote travel books that, *mirabile dictu*, still find readers and have appreciated in value; and who even composed an Oxford Prize Essay in the cabin of a steamer on the Nile.

Sometimes, as I recall those days, I find myself reviving memories or telling tales that seem to belong to a past that is quite dead, not merely by reason of the change in my own environment, but also because of the revolution in the conditions of travel, or in the state of the peoples and lands which I visited. For instance, in some countries where I rode thousands of weary miles on horseback, the traveller now proceeds rapidly and comfortably by carriage or motor, or even by train. In other countries – as, for instance, Korea, which at the time of my visit in 1892 was still independent and had a Court and a King – political changes have brought about a transformation not less startling. And so it comes into my mind that there may be something in the experiences of those days that may be worthy of record before I have forgotten them, and which other people will perhaps not have the chance of repeating in the same way.

The following pages contain these memories. They have nothing to do with politics. They relate to many parts of the world, but principally to the East, which has always been to me the source of inspiration and ideas. Most of the papers are of no great length, and only a few are learned. Whether I ought to advertise or to apologise for the latter must be left to the judgment of my readers. All relate to places or incidents lying somewhat outside the ordinary run of travel. Had I written a volume of political memoirs, could I have hoped to escape controversy? As it is, nothing that I have set down will, I trust, excite dispute. The genuine traveller quarrels with nobody – except his predecessors or rivals, a temptation which I have been careful to avoid. All countries are his washpot. All mankind is his friend.

Perhaps the most striking testimony that I could offer to the change that has passed over the scenes of my earlier journeys – and incidentally also to the chronically unstable equilibrium of the East – would be a reference to the dramatic fate that has befallen so many of the rulers and statesmen with whom I was brought in contact, and some of whom appear in these pages, in the days to which I refer. Shah Nasr-ed-Din of Persia, my audience with whom at Teheran in 1889 is mentioned later on,

The dramatic fate that has befallen so many of the rulers and statesmen that I met, among them:

The Emperor of Annam was forced to abdicate (bottom left). Abbas Hilmi, a fugitive and an exile (top right).

The mad King of Bavaria, who ended by drowning himself in the lake (top left).

King George of Greece, who came to his death at the hand of an assassin (bottom right).

perished in 1896 by the weapon of an assassin. The ruler of Chitral with whom I stayed in 1894 was shot and killed by the half-brother who had sat at table with him and me only two months before. The Emperor of Annam, who presented me with a golden decoration at Hué in 1892, first saw his Queen murdered in the Palace and was afterwards himself forced to abdicate. His son, who struck me as the stupidest young man I ever met, shared the same fate. Deposition was the fate of the trembling figure of Norodom, the King of Cambodia, whom I visited at Pnompenh. The Amir of Bokhara, whom I saw in his capital in 1888, was afterwards expelled from his country and throne. Abbas Hilmi, whom Lord Cromer took me to visit at Cairo, soon after he had ascended the Khedivial throne, is also a fugitive and an exile.

The life of that eminent Japanese statesman, the Marquis Ito, who was so friendly to me when I was in Japan, was cut short by the knife of an assassin. Almost alone among the Eastern potentates whose guest I was, the Amir Abdur Rahman Khan, who told me that he lived in daily fear of his life, but that his people had not the courage to kill him, died in his bed. But of his two sons with whom I used to dine at Kabul, the elder, Habibulla, was murdered in his tent, and the younger, Nasrulla, languishes in prison. His Commander-in-Chief, known as the Sipah Salar, a gigantic figure, 6 feet 3 inches in height, and of corresponding bulk, who rode at my side from Dacca to Jellalabad on my way to Kabul in 1904, died suddenly a few years later in circumstances which left little doubt that his end was not natural.

Even in Europe my diaries refer to more than one similar tragedy. As far back as 1880 I recall a visit to the picturesque castle of Herrenhausen in Bavaria, where, in a room adorned exclusively with furniture and decorations in the shape of swans, I heard the steady tramp overhead, as he passed to and fro, of the mad King of Bavaria, who ended by drowning himself in a lake. I recall very clearly, and others have related, the incidents of a dinner with King George of Greece, who came to his death at the hand of an assassin in the streets of Salonika.

These incidents illustrate no more uncommon phenomenon than that the lives of monarchs and statesmen are subject to exceptional and fatal risks, particularly in the East. But as I recall the features and tones of those ill-fated victims, so famous or so prominent in their day, a chasm appears to open between me and the time when I saw them in the plenitude of their strength and power – and I seem to be almost living in a world of different circumstances and different men.

I have said that this volume is intended to be descriptive rather than didactic in object, and that I hope not so much to instruct as to entertain. But a few of my subjects may be thought to make a more sober claim, or to demand a more definite apology. The portrait of the Afghan Amir, with whom I was the only Englishman to stay at Kabul in a private and unofficial capacity, is the likeness of one of the most remarkable men of his time – a man who, had he lived in an earlier age and not been crushed, as he told me, like an earthenware pot between the rival forces of England and Russia, might have founded an Empire, and swept in a tornado of

The Amir Abdur Rahman Khan, who lived in daily fear of his life.

Crossing the Himalayan rope-bridge, sagging in the middle and swaying dizzily from side to side.

blood over Asia and even beyond it.

There are many other aspects of travel, apart from its incidents or experiences, which I should like to examine, but which must be deferred to a later volume. Among these is a study of the Philosophy of Travel – its character, history, purpose, methods, justification, and results; and a chapter or more on the Literature of Travel – a subject that, to the best of my knowledge, has never received attention save perhaps in the casual pages of a magazine.

Here, however, I conclude with a reflection that will certainly not offend by its seriousness. The joy of travel, while it is being pursued, lies in a good many things: in the observation of new peoples and scenes, in the making of discoveries, in the zest of sport or adventure, in the pleasures of companionship or the excitement of new acquaintances, even in the collection of often valueless objects, and the achievement of purely illusory bargains. But I think that even more does it consist in the half-intangible but still positive memories that it leaves. One can make friends with places as well as people; and an hour's, even a minute's, experience in one spot may be more precious than a sojourn of months in another. These are the intimacies that survive, and constitute a perpetual endowment. With them we can always solace the hours, whether of idleness or gloom.

Whereas the experiences of life at home, even when they are not commonplace, are apt to fade quickly, and sometimes to be completely forgotten, the incidents of travel, a quarter or even half of a century ago, stand out indelibly as though graven in steel. Each of us has his own museum of such recollections. Among mine not the least prized are these: the music of many nightingales floating across the water from the coasts of Athos; the incredible glory of Kangchenjunga as he pierces the veils of the morning at Darjiling; the crossing of a Himalayan rope-bridge, sagging in the middle, and swaying dizzily from side to side, when only a strand of twisted twigs is stretched between your feet and the ravening torrent below; the first sight of the towered walls, minae murorum ingentes, of Peking; the head and shoulders of an Indian tiger emerging without a suspicion of sound from the thick jungle immediately in front of the posted sportsmen; the stupendous and terraced grandeur of Angkor Wat; the snowy spire of Teneriffe glimmering at sunrise across a hundred miles of ocean; the aethereal and ineffable beauty of the Taj.

I am not going to trouble my readers by saying anything about these particular mind-pictures in this book. I merely record them in passing, as a part of my own spiritual possession, just as others will have and will cherish theirs. The things that I have preferred to set down here are experiences or memories rather less personal and fugitive, which I may be justified in inviting others, even though on paper and in print only, to share, and which, here and there, may give them a few moments of entertainment or reflection.

Discoveries

We were the first that ever burst
Into that silent sea.
COLERIDGE, *Ancient Mariner.*

And things are not what they seem.
LONGFELLOW, *Psalm of Life.*

IT is quite a mistake to suppose that the era of discovery is over, and that no more secrets of history or nature are to be wrested from the face of the earth by the observant pilgrim. Travel is still the science of the unexpected and the unknown, at least to those who know how to pursue it; and it is far from necessary to go either to Lhasa or Timbuctoo in order to learn things that one has never previously imagined, or to see sights of uncommon novelty and interest.

In the course of many years of travel, I never made so many discoveries as during the first journey that I took, when a very young man, to Egypt, Palestine, and Syria. There seemed, indeed, to be something in the atmosphere of those countries that was peculiarly favourable to this sort of exploration; and I can still recall the delight with which day after day I saw new planets swim into my ken – planets of the very existence or place of which in the geographical firmament I had not previously been aware.

I had received some measure of preparation for my subsequent discoveries by a preliminary tour in Egypt, where, from the day on which I landed, these experiences began. Thus at Alexandria, where I had always been led to believe that the great Pompey had been murdered and his body left exposed on the beach, I made the immediate discovery that Pompey's Pillar had nothing to do with the real Pompey, but was an old Egyptian shaft fitted with a capital and base of inferior classical design by another and obscure Pompey, two hundred and fifty years later, in honour of the Emperor Diocletian. This did not disturb me greatly; because I had already realised that Cleopatra's two needles, one of which had been transferred to America and the other to London, had never been threaded by that fascinating lady, and had, indeed, been set up at least 1800 years before she was born. And if Cleopatra was to be made the victim of a clumsy lie, why not Pompey also?

But my discoveries about Cleopatra did not end here; for when I saw her portrait, carved on the back wall of the Temple of Denderah, I realised either that her beauty must have been as great a mystery as that of Mary Queen of Scots, or else that the Egyptian portrait-sculptors of the day were very inferior artists (probably this particular artist never saw the Queen, and produced a merely conventional profile), or that the recorded history of her triumphs must be a myth. Anyhow, it was a discovery; although it did not alter my personal conviction that Cleopatra was a very beautiful woman, that her skin was white, whether her hair was light or dark, and that her features were pure Greek (why, indeed, seeing that she

Alexandria, where I had always been led to believe that the great Pompey had been murdered.

came of a Greek stock who propagated the race by close intermarriage, should she have been anything else?), and that the woman who beguiled both Caesar and Antony, ruining the one and very nearly ruining the other, was worthy of her achievements.

Furthermore, I comforted myself by the reflection that the Egyptian atmosphere had never been very favourable to truth. In the book of Exodus there are traces of exaggeration, if not worse. Herodotus, the Father of History, had made some startling discoveries in Egypt and had been told a good many lies by the Egyptians; he had also himself told a few more, and perhaps this had set the ball rolling; so that Egypt had acquired a reputation in these respects which it was necessary to sustain, and which, I am bound to say, its inhabitants up to the latest hour have never done anything to impair.

From that time forward I never felt or expressed astonishment at any discovery of the kind which I was fortunate enough to make, but merely recorded it with delight in my note-book. For instance, when I came to Assouan I found with no surprise that the First Cataract of the Nile, even as it then existed, was not a cataract at all, but only a rapid a few yards wide, with a fall in 150 yards of not more than six or seven feet. But then Herodotus also made a discovery about this same cataract; for hereabouts were his two famous hills of Crophi and Mophi, between which lay the unfathomable fountains of the Nile.

It was not, however, till I passed on to Palestine and Syria that I realised that there the real field of original discovery lay. Already I knew enough to be aware that the roses of Sharon were not roses, that the Palestine lilies of the field which "toiled not neither did they spin" were not lilies, and that the milk and honey with which the country was reported to flow, were neither the produce of the cow nor the manufacture of the bee. But this knowledge was nothing to that which I was destined in a few weeks to acquire.

The First Cataract of the Nile was not a cataract at all.

Some of these discoveries were quite innocent, and were no doubt the result of culpable previous ignorance on my own part. For instance, when I climbed to the Place of Sacrifice on Mount Carmel, which I had fondly imagined to be a grassy eminence on the summit of a lofty hill overlooking the Mediterranean, whence the servant of the prophet saw arising "a little cloud out of the sea, like a man's hand", it was a genuine discovery to learn that the actual site (which cannot, I believe, be disputed) was at the south-east and landward extremity of a ridge, twelve miles long, from which neither Haifa nor Acre could be seen, and where only a little patch of sea was visible to the west and south at the distance of many miles.

Again I had been a good deal disappointed with the sight of the River Jordan, which I crossed at Jericho without dismounting from my horse – it was little larger than a brook. But I waited for Damascus, knowing that

Abana and Pharpar, rivers of Damascus, were better than all the waters of Israel. That they might easily be, though I found them to be only swift but narrow snow-fed rivulets, flowing through the town to which they supply water for every use. Even when I read my Kinglake, whom I believed to be a truthful man, I hardly recovered my confidence:

This Holy Damascus, this "Earthly Paradise" of the Prophet, so fair to the eyes that he dared not trust himself to tarry in her blissful shades, she is a city of hidden palaces, of copses, and gardens, and fountains, and bubbling streams. The juice of her lips is the gushing and ice-cold torrent that tumbles from the snowy sides of Anti-Lebanon. Close along the river's edge, through seven sweet miles of rustling boughs and deepest shade, the city spreads out her whole length; as a man falls flat, face forward, on the brook that he may drink and drink again, so Damascus, thirsting for ever, lies down with her lips to the stream and clings to its rushing waters.

I always thought this very beautiful. But I found that the beauty lay in the exquisite music of *Eothen* rather than in the scene itself.

It was, however, in respect of the established sacred sites that my more exciting discoveries lay. I experienced no surprise, indeed, at learning that there is hardly a place or scene in the Old or New Testament which has not been identified with scrupulous accuracy. Thus, to see the House of Joseph, or the Tomb of the Virgin, or the Sarcophagus of David, or the burial-place of Nicodemus, or the home of the kindly man by whom Paul

Damascus, thirsting for ever, lies down with her lips to the stream.

was let down in a basket and who is known as George the Porter, or even the spot where the cock crew to Peter, were sensations that might well have been foreseen. Nor, when I came to the Moslem Sacred Sites, was I greatly startled to be shown the round hole in the rock, inside the Mosque of Omar at Jerusalem, through which Mohammed rose to heaven on the back of his athletic steed, or even the fragments of the saddle which that animal bore, although this saddle was rather unexpectedly made of marble. Further, I had not known beforehand that the rock itself was only prevented from following the Prophet in his aerial flight by the special intervention of the Archangel Gabriel, whose finger-prints are still visible where he held it down.

But what I had altogether failed to anticipate was that the most famous men of the Scriptures, with an admirable regard for the convenience of posterity, should have concentrated their main activities on approximately the same site or sites. Thus, after I had exhausted the sights of the Holy Sepulchre, it was a great relief to know that without leaving the building I could see both the grave of Adam, who, I thought, had ended his days at some considerable distance, and the place where Abraham attempted to sacrifice Isaac; whilst in the dome of the rock Mohammed had struck his head against the ceiling so hard that he left an unmistakable impression side by side with the place – also unmistakable – where David and Solomon had prayed.

All these discoveries, however, paled before the realisation that in Palestine and Syria men could be buried several times over without

exciting any surprise. It is true that I had read in England of two, if not three, well-attested skulls of Oliver Cromwell, and that I was familiar with the explanation given by the owner of one of these to the visitor who complained that he had already seen the skull of the Protector elsewhere, and that it was a good deal bigger. "Oh, but our skull", had been the reply, "was the skull of Oliver Cromwell when he was a little boy."

I was therefore prepared for some uncertainty about the relics of the dead. Moreover, I realised that there might be some reason for a double record in the case of Lazarus, whose tomb I encountered first at Bethany, and afterwards at Larnaka in Cyprus. Again, we know that John the Baptist was beheaded; which may explain how it came about that I saw the mausoleum of his body at Samaria, and of his head at Damascus. But it did not explain how, on another occasion, I came across the greater part of his remains at Genoa in Italy. The Virgin Mary had also two graves, one in the Garden in Gethsemane, and another at Ephesus (with the tomb of St. John thrown in). But the hero of the greatest achievement was undoubtedly Noah. It is true that history contains no record of the stages by which he trekked from Ararat to the Holy Land. But let that pass – for it was only a minor discovery in comparison with others. I had, I thought, already left him safely buried at Hebron, when later on, in the neighbourhood of Baalbek, I came upon him again; and this time he was interred in a tomb forty yards long by two or three feet wide, thereby throwing an entirely new light upon the methods by which he may have escaped the Flood, without ever building or entering the Ark. Noah must, as I say, have been a person of exceptional stature, even in a part of the world where the Sons of Anak, "which come of the giants", and compared with whom all other men "were as grasshoppers", would appear to have abounded. But even in his day the standard of human height must have been rapidly deteriorating; for the grave of Eve, near Jeddah in the Hejaz, which corresponds accurately to the dimensions of her body, is no less than 173 yards long by 12 yards wide; so that compared with the ancestral Mother of Mankind, the builder of the Ark was only a pigmy. At Jeddah, however, the guardians of her tomb have a ready and indeed plausible explanation of this decline, for they say that when Eve fell, with her fell the stature of the race which she originated.

Such are a few only of the manifold and gratifying discoveries that I made while journeying on the eastern shores of the Mediterranean forty years ago; and though I have never in any of my subsequent wanderings maintained the same high level of accomplishment, they justify me, I think, in claiming that travel, even in modern times, is still capable of adding immensely, and sometimes unexpectedly, to the sum total of human knowledge.

A double record in the case of Lazarus, whose tomb I encountered twice.

Curzon of Kedleston
1900 –

The Top Hat at Teheran

The hat is the *ultimum moriens* of respectability.

O. WENDELL HOLMES,
The Autocrat of the Breakfast Table viii.

WHEN I was at Teheran in the autumn of 1889, as the guest of the British Minister, Sir H. Drummond Wolff, the latter procured for me an audience with H.M. Nasr-ed-Din Shah. But for this purpose I was informed that a black silk top hat such as we wear in the streets of London was indispensable. Now, though I should never think of travelling either to Timbuctoo or even the North Pole without a dress suit – for in anxious circumstances this is a recognised hallmark of respectability throughout the world, and will procure an audience of almost any living potentate – I had not encumbered myself in my Persian journeys, where all my effects had to be strapped on to the back of a horse, galloping sixty or seventy miles in the day, with anything so perishable as a top hat. Nor was such an object to be found for love or money in the shops of Teheran.

The British and other foreign Legations were ransacked for what they might be able to produce in the shape of the obligatory headpiece; but, although a few somewhat battered specimens were forthcoming, the diplomatic cranium generally appeared to be of so ill-developed a character, at any rate as represented at that time in the Persian capital, that not one of them could I persuade to rest upon my head, which happens to be unduly large and round. I amused myself by repeating the famous remark of Jowett in his funeral sermon upon Dean Stanley, which I had heard when an undergraduate at Balliol some years before, when the Master had said that though mitres rained upon Stanley as thick as hailstones from heaven, his head was so curiously shaped that none of them would precisely fit it.

The British Minister himself had a head of creditable dimensions; and I found by experiment that his hat, which was decent though tarnished, could be comfortably fitted on my brow. But alas! when I suggested that he should surrender it to me and go to the audience – for he was to present me – in his cocked hat and diplomatic uniform, he absolutely declined to do anything so subversive of the official etiquette at a private audience. His top hat was his own, and upon no other head should it repose.

Amid this sequence of cruel disappointments the time sped rapidly by until the eve of the day of audience arrived.

No top hat had yet been procured, and I contemplated the probability of having to go bare-headed through the streets, a not too enviable experience under a midday Asiatic sun.

On the very last evening, however, a young Persian Minister had invited me to dinner at his house in the Persian style, to which a few other Europeans had also been bidden. We passed a very pleasant evening, and tasted rather than consumed an immense number of succulent Persian

The obligatory headpiece which I persuaded to rest upon my head.

I should never think of travelling either to Timbuctoo or even the North Pole without a dress suit.

dishes; among the company being a French *savant* of world-wide reputation, who had arrived at Teheran in the pursuit of certain anthropological researches. As we left the house at a late hour – the party to which I belonged being the first to go – and passed through the vestibule, I started with an exclamation of almost rapturous surprise when I beheld standing upon the table, prominent and inviting, a black silk hat, glossy, capacious and new. With a presence of mind on which I have never ceased to congratulate myself, I clapped it on to my head, over which it came down nearly to the ears, ran out of the house, jumped on to my horse, and returned at full gallop to the British Legation.

On the next afternoon I was duly presented to His Majesty the Shah, my top hat being the admiration of all observers, and in the evening the headpiece was returned, with profuse apologies for the slight mistake, to the learned *savant*. He is doubtless unaware to this hour that but for his head and his hat I should never have had the honour of an audience with H.M. Nasr-ed-Din Shah.

The Annamite Girl

I am black but comely.
Song of Solomon, i.5.

———————⊙———————

WHEN I came back from one of my long journeys in the East, in the course of which I had visited the French possessions of Tongking, Annam and Cochin-China, I delivered a lecture at the Royal Geographical Society on the subject of my travels. The meeting was held in the Theatre of the University of London in Burlington Gardens, and was honoured by the presence of King Edward VII, then Prince of Wales, who occupied a seat upon the platform. Every bench from floor to roof was filled, and many people were turned away. At the end of my paper the illustrations which I had selected from a large number of photographs, either taken by myself or collected during my tour, were thrown from a lantern on to the screen, each slide being preceded by a brief explanatory description from myself. All went well until, after exhibiting slides of the scenery and buildings of Tongking, I said, "I will now show you the picture of an Annamite girl, in order to prove that the native population, though possessing marked Mongolian features, are far from destitute of personal charm. Indeed," I added, "I thought some of them quite pretty."

King Edward VII, then Prince of Wales, occupied a seat upon the platform.

29

An Annamite girl who though possessing marked Mongolian features is far from destitute of personal charm.

All eyes were turned upon the screen, upon which there forthwith appeared, magnified to far more than life size, the figure of a seated Annamite girl, destitute of any but the smallest shred of clothing.

The audience, after a slight pause of bewildered surprise, burst into roars of laughter, again and again renewed, in which His Royal Highness heartily joined; nor did he ever cease to chaff me afterwards about my Annamite lady friend. No explanation availed anything. It was useless for me to declare – though it was the strict truth – that the photograph was one of a packet which had been presented to me by the Governor-General of French Indo-China, in order to illustrate the people and habits of that country, and that I had incautiously handed the entire packet, with marks upon those which were to be put upon the slides, to the lantern operator, who in a spirit, as I imagine, of mischief, had ignored my instructions and selected this unmarked photograph for reproduction.

No one believed me. But from the moment that the figure of the young girl was thrown upon the screen the success of the lecture was assured, in the same hour that the character of the lecturer was irreparably destroyed.

The State Entry into Koweit

They have their exits and their entrances.
SHAKESPEARE, *As You Like It*, Act II. Scene VII.

———◦❈◦———

MY official entry into Koweit, at the head of the Persian Gulf, in November 1903, was of a character somewhat different from the less orthodox entry into Kabul, which I have before described. But it was not without its vicissitudes.

I was the first Viceroy of India to visit Koweit, and the Sheikh Mubarrak, with whom I had recently concluded a secret treaty of friendly alliance on behalf of His Majesty's Government, and who was himself a striking and powerful type of Arab chieftain, was anxious to treat me with becoming honour.

This desire on his part demanded a ceremonial entry into the capital of his State; and in order that this might be accomplished with becoming display, it was necessary that, instead of landing at the town itself, which is built on the shore of the Gulf, our party should be taken in boats to a point about three miles away, where we could land on a shelving spit of sand and be escorted from thence to the town. As we neared the landing-place I observed that the Sheikh with his principal retainers and a great crowd of mounted Arabs were assembled on the shore to greet me, and that in front of the crowd was a small open vehicle or Victoria, drawn by a pair of Arab horses and evidently intended for the accommodation of the Sheikh and myself. I was informed that this was the first time that such a vehicle had ever been seen at Koweit, and that it had been specially ordered by the Sheikh from Bombay to do honour to his visitor.

Accordingly, after exchanging the customary *salaams*, the Sheikh and I entered the equipage, which set off at a brisk trot for the town, escorted by the camel corps of twelve to twenty men, and by some two hundred to two hundred and fifty horsemen. Some of these wore helmets and coats of chain mail. The Sheikh's flag, with the timely inscription "Trust in God" sewn in white on a scarlet background, was carried in front.

Meanwhile the whole of my staff, including the British Minister at Teheran, who accompanied me, were provided with Arab mounts, the tall peaked saddles of which, with the shovel stirrups, are not always conducive to the comfort or even to the security of riders unused to them.

However, everyone climbed up in due course, and the procession moved off in a cloud of dust. At this stage it apparently became necessary for the cavalry escort to express their rejoicing not merely by war-cries of the most blood-curdling description, but by firing ball cartridge promiscuously either in the air or into the ground at the feet of their prancing steeds. Others hurled their spears frantically into the air. The result was the wildest confusion. The air resounded with the fusillade, and the ground was a whirlwind of careering horses and yelling cavaliers and spurting sand. Some of the horsemen were bare-headed, and their plaited

OVERLEAF
My official entry into Koweit.

In order that this might be accomplished with becoming display, it was necessary that we land on a shelving spit of sand.

A small open vehicle or Victoria, evidently intended for my accommodation.

I entered the equipage escorted by the camel corps of twelve to twenty men.

hair streamed in the wind as they dashed along; others wore flowing garments of orange and red and golden brown. The chief was clad in a broad-striped robe.

In the midst of the scene I saw the form of the British Minister shot clean over the head of his steed and deposited with no small violence upon the ground. Nothing daunted, he courageously resumed his seat and, amid a hail of bullets, continued the uneven tenor of his way.

As we approached the town, we passed through the entire population (the bazaars having been closed for the day), who were ranged in two rows on either side of our route. The prevailing colour of their men's dress was dark brown, but all wore the white Arab keffyeh with the twisted camel hair bound round the head. Behind them stood the women, closely veiled and with their figures concealed in dark indigo cloaks of an almost funereal appearance, below which were skirts of gaudy cotton prints. As the cortege passed they indulged in a shrill wail or series of ululations, which might have been mistaken for a dirge of exceptional poignancy, were it not that, as I learned, the sounds were intended to express the extremity of rapture and joy.

Thus escorted, we presently reached the so-called palace of the Sheikh, a modest edifice, built for the most part of sun-dried bricks and situated in a very narrow street or lane of the town. We climbed to the first floor of this building for the exchange of the customary courtesies, accompanied by coffee and cigarettes, of Arab etiquette.

As I sat there, bandying civilities with my host, a sound of violent rending and tearing, accompanied by loud shouts and plunging of horse-hoofs, broke the solemn hush of our palaver. Not a word was said on the subject. But when the interview was over and I descended to the street, only the fragments of the Bombay Victoria, reduced to matchwood, littered the ground, and the steeds had vanished! It appeared that these animals, who had never before been harnessed to a vehicle, had made up for their orderly behaviour, while conducting the Sheikh and myself from the landing-place to the town, by kicking the somewhat flimsy construction to pieces as soon as they were left alone. I doubt if a Victoria has been seen in Koweit since.

We had to feel our way very gingerly on foot over heaps of ordure and amid indescribable filth to a nearer point of embarkation for our vessel, which was lying at anchor at a considerable distance in the shallow waters of the Gulf. Thus began and thus ignobly ended my Viceregal entry into Koweit.

The Young Judge

O wise young judge, how I do honour thee.
SHAKESPEARE, *Merchant of Venice*, Act IV. Sc. 1.

———◦❈◦———

THE death of King Victor Emmanuel in January 1878 produced an immense sensation throughout Italy, where he was not merely regarded as the national hero who had re-established the national unity, and placed Italy once more in the front rank of states, but had endeared himself to the people by his sporting instincts, his indomitable gallantries, and his interest in the life of all classes of the population. The title "Il Re Galantuomo" fitly represented the national conception both of his character and his service. The demonstrations of sorrow were universal and sincere, and all Italy yearned to testify its sense of the irreparable loss which the nation had sustained. Inasmuch as the whole of the country could not participate in the obsequies at Rome, where the King had been buried, it was decided to hold a great ceremony for Northern Italy at Milan, where a service was announced to be held in the Duomo, and a Requiem Mass performed. Tens of thousands of persons poured into Milan from all parts of the country, and the city was as packed as though, instead of conducting a service over a man already interred elsewhere, the body of the King himself was to be carried by his mourning people to the actual grave.

I happened to be in Milan with my old and trusted friend Oscar Browning; and we considered in what way we could, without any special credentials, see the spectacle and take part in the celebration. We decided in any case to put on black evening clothes, top hats, and white ties, as likely to be in harmony with the sentiment of the hour. Thus attired we sallied out in the morning and made our way through the crowded streets to the Prefecture to see if we could obtain permission to enter the Cathedral. There was a great crowd round the official building, where processions of provincial mayors and district judges were being organised, and were in some cases already starting on their way. Observing that some of these gentlemen were garbed in raiment almost identical with our own, we insinuated ourselves in their midst, and walked with admirable composure in their company through the long covered gallery or arcade that leads into the Piazza before the Duomo. O. B.'s fluent command of Italian enabled him to cope easily with the situation. But I was a little embarrassed when my neighbour in the procession addressed me with the remark that I appeared to be an exceptionally youthful Judge, and wanted to know whence I came. I acknowledged the precocity, but refrained from otherwise adding to his information.

At length we emerged into the great Piazza, which was filled with an enormous crowd, and, crossing this, marched up the main steps of the Duomo and entered by the central door. At the head of the nave stood a gigantic catafalque on which rested the empty coffin, draped in purple

I happened to be in Milan with my old and trusted friend Oscar Browning (right).

and black, that represented the absent body of the King. Whether the illusion that we were Judges did or did not continue to prevail, at any rate no one obstructed our passage to the foot of the catafalque, where the bishops assisting in the ceremony took their seats at our feet. From this vantage ground we witnessed without interruption the entire ceremony.

It was not free from tragedy. For after the processions had entered and the service had already advanced far on its way, the crowd in the Piazza, who had not been permitted to enter the Cathedral, burst through the great door that closed the northern side aisle and flocked into the building. Like a flood they poured up the aisle, climbing the monuments, overturning the occupants of the seats, and crushing and trampling each other under foot. A part of the Mass was being chanted by a tenor with a divine voice, whose name was Tommaso or Tommasino (or some such name); but loud above his glorious notes rang through the marble colonnades the agonising shrieks of the tortured men and women. The next day we read in the papers that not a few persons had been crushed to death in that desperate and almost demoniacal struggle.

The Dancing Girl of Keneh

Take her up tenderly,
Lift her with care;
Fashioned so slenderly,
Young and so fair.
T. HOOD, "The Bridge of Sighs".

THE dance was over. We had looked on at the contortions and wrigglings, the undulations and oscillations of the bodies of the girls as they performed on the deck of the boat. So violent had been their movements that the coins which hung on their gauzy dresses rattled and rang. The usual accompaniment had been furnished by the castanets of the dancers, the two-string cocoa-nut fiddle of the seated musicians, and the thrumming of the *darabookah*, or native drum. One of the girls, more agile than her companions, had lain down on the carpet and rolled over and over with a champagne bottle on her head containing a lighted candle stuck in its neck.

The company, departing for their native village of Keneh, famed for its school of dancers, had to cross a narrow plank between the steamer and the steep bank of the Nile. Suddenly a cry was raised that one of them, either jostled as she stepped ashore, or slipping on the plank, had fallen overboard. Looking over the side of the boat and listening to the confused noise in the bows, I saw something black float by on the surface of the water a few feet away. Little as I guessed at the moment, this was the head and hair of the drowning girl, who had gone without a struggle or a sound to her doom.

Quickly lowering a boat, we pulled down stream and lifted out the body 150 yards farther down.

On the muddy bank, lit only by the flicker of a solitary lantern and the remote glitter of the stars, lay the poor child's body, the head thrown back, the brown bosom bare, the bedraggled finery clinging round the limbs that half an hour before had tripped and twisted and turned. For three-quarters of an hour we endeavoured in vain to restore respiration amid the piercing cries of the other members of the troupe. It was of no use. One more unfortunate had gone to her death, and the Nile – a very fatal current into which to fall – had claimed another victim. I collected £10 on board and sent it to the Mudir of Keneh for distribution to the girl's relatives. But so handsome was the price, or so tempting the bribe, that when we came down stream again a deputation from Keneh awaited us to implore the favour of another performance.

The Arab Runaway at Nejef

Asshur shall not save us; we will not ride upon horses.
Hosea xiv.3.

THE holy shrine of Nejef, one of the two most sacred places of the Shiah faith, situated in the Arabian desert, was my destination. There I was to be the guest of a learned *Mujtahed* or Mussulman Doctor of the Law, bearing the appropriate and high-sounding title of the Bahru' l' Ulum, or Sea of Science; and he had commissioned his brother, a demure and courtly Seyid, to greet me and bring me to the city. It was very cold in the early morning. In the distance on the left the tower of Birs Nimrud peered above a blue sea of vapour which enveloped the lower part of the great *tepe* or mound of burnt bricks from which it springs. Immense flocks of wild geese rose with loud clamour from the surrounding marshes and flew in a perfect cunei-form formation, behind their squadron leader, at a great height in the sky.

Not a sign of human life or habitation broke the stark monotony of the desert. But as the sun climbed above the horizon, a spark of fire, dwindling and then glowing again, scintillated on the skyline, where the rays of the mounting orb splintered on the golden dome of Nejef.

The Seyid and I were riding side by side, and I was receiving instruction from him in the history and mysteries of the sacred places, when there approached us a gaily caparisoned cavalcade, in the midst of which curvetted and caracoled a magnificent white Arab steed. On his back were a velvet saddle-cloth, and a high-peaked Arab saddle, studded with silver; and the heavy shovel-stirrups, hanging loose at his side, jangled to and fro as he leaped and pranced. The two parties met; and thereupon I learned that this splendid animal, the private property of the Seyid, and the prize inmate of his stable, had been sent out by my host, in order that on his back I might make a becoming entry into the sacred city.

To me, however (I am not ashamed to confess), the prospect of exchanging my good horse and English saddle for the doubtful amenities of the Arab equipment and the exuberant frolics of this impassioned steed, made no appeal; and I felt a shrewd suspicion that my entry into the site of such holy memories, if honourable, would also be rapid. I recalled the unhappy experience of the Cardinal Balue in the pages of *Quentin Durward*, and I was resolved to escape a similar fate. With extreme civility, therefore, I pressed upon the Seyid the consideration that the laws of courtesy did not permit me to deprive him of his own horse, and that I should regard it as the highest honour to ride at his side into the town. I urged him therefore to exchange the animal that he was riding for this more showy mount. Although he displayed almost as much reluctance as I had done to make the exchange, he presently consented, and proceeded to dismount.

No sooner, however, had he placed one foot in the huge shovel-stirrup,

The holy shrine of Nejef, one of the two most sacred places of the Shiah faith.

hardly had the other leg swung in the air over the pointed crupper than, like an arrow from the bow, the proud Arab was off into the desert. No Derby winner ever covered the course at Epsom in more approved style or at a more headlong speed. I can see the steed and his rider now, the white mane and long tail of the horse stretched taut, the brown *aba* or cloak of the Seyid bellying and streaming (like the purple coat of the Cardinal) in the wind, his snow-white turban swaying over the head of the runaway, the thud of hoofs growing fainter and fainter on the hard gravel of the desert, as horse and rider disappeared into the void. In almost less time than it has taken to write these sentences, they were a speck on the horizon, and finally vanished altogether from view. Nor, until I entered the gates of the city, did the holy man reappear, flushed and pouring with perspiration, but mounted on another and less fiery steed.

On the next morning, after seeing the sights of the place, we rode out through the high walls of the town on our way to the mosque of Kufa, five miles distant. The Seyid still did me the honour of accompanying me; but this time I observed that he was mounted on a fine white female donkey, behind which trotted a young foal. When I asked him why he did not ride his own beautiful horse, he replied that he would mount it a little outside the city. Later on he said that the exchange would be effected at Kufa. But Kufa came and was passed. Kifl came, Birs Nimrud came, and before sundown we had reached Babylon. But still the secure and patient ass bore the form of the prudent Seyid of Nejef, and the not less prudent Englishman on his Baghdadi horse and his English saddle rode contentedly at his side.

A Duel

Honour pricks me on. Yea, but how if honour prick me off when I come
on? how then? Can honour set to a leg? no: or an arm? no: or take away
the grief of a wound? no. Honour hath no skill in surgery, then? no.
SHAKESPEARE, *King Henry IV*, Part I. Act V. Sc. 1.

I could not love thee, dear, so much,
Loved I not honour more.
RICHARD LOVELACE, *To Lucasta*.

WE had foregathered at Jerusalem. It was a quite accidental combina-
tion. Five young men, drawn to Palestine by the lure of travel, bent upon
seeing and enjoying all that they could. They included a wealthy young
American, two English clergymen, one of them a curate in the East End
of London, a Harvard student from U.S.A., and a young English traveller, to wit, myself. We had abundance of spirits, sound health, no cares,
and a passion to explore and enjoy. It was in the year 1883.

We saw and did all the familiar and some unfamiliar things in Palestine. We bathed in the Jordan and the Sea of Galilee. Making the trip to
Jericho, we assisted in a native fantasia organised there in honour of J. M.
Cook, the head of the famous firm of Thomas Cook & Sons, who was just
then opening up Palestine as an area of his agencies, and whom we saw
hoisted round the camp at night with a torchlight procession by a crowd
of shrieking Arabs, grateful for the anticipated fall of manna in the
wilderness which he was expected to ensure. I doubt if Jericho had seen
any more curious sight since its walls fell down some considerable time
ago.

Together we climbed Ebal and Gerizim, Tabor and Carmel. Together
we bought exquisitely enamelled tiles at Damascus, having a raffle and
casting dice for four lovely pieces, because none of us had the money to
buy the lot except the American, who, of course, won the competition.
Together we were photographed on horseback on the great stone, par-
tially hewn, but still unsevered from its quarry bed, at Baalbek.

At Beyrout we took passage in a densely crowded Austrian Lloyd boat,
where we five were crammed into a single cabin of small dimensions. The
etiquette of behaviour on this boat was prescribed by the following polite
admonition, which was posted in more than one conspicuous place in the
ship:

Passengers having a right to be treated like persons of education will,
no doubt, conform themselves to the rules of good society by respecting
their fellow-travellers, and paying a due regard to the fair sex.

Being young and gallant, we endeavoured faithfully to observe both
parts of this injunction. But we avenged ourselves on the Company which
had incarcerated us in this marine Black Hole in the following ingenious

*We bought exquisitely enamelled
tiles at Damascus.*

41

fashion. The American student had a very good tenor voice, and had been a chorus-leader at Harvard, of all the songs and chants of which admirable institution he was an acknowledged master. Nightly, our party, known as the Goats – in contradistinction to the remainder of the passengers, whose higher level of piety and decorum entitled them to be called the Sheep – gave an open-air concert on deck, of which the most popular feature was an American student song (sung to the tune of "Auld Lang Syne"), each verse being given out in advance by the Choragus, and then shouted in lusty unison by the entire audience. I remember some verses of this jovial lay.

> There was a farmer had two sons,
>   And these two sons were brothers!
> Josephus was the eldest's name,
>   Bohuncus was the other's.

> Now these two boys had suits of clothes
>   They bought for Easter Sunday;
> Josephus wore his all the week,
>   Bohuncus on the Monday.

> Now these two boys had an old horse,
>   And this old horse was blind;
> Josephus rode him up before,
>   Bohuncus down behind.

> Now these two brothers died at last,
>   It grieves me sore to tell,
> Josephus up to heaven went,
>   Bohuncus down to –.

This finale was yelled with extreme gusto by every one on board, except the missionaries, who usually retired before the climax was reached.

Our revenge upon the Company was effected by the introduction nightly of an improvised stanza reflecting upon the scant hospitality of the vessel and the disgraceful overcrowding of which we were the victims. I recall one of these verses:

> These brothers sailed in an Austrian Lloyd,
>   They never will again!
> Josephus had five in his berth,
>   Bohuncus was with ten.

Other verses were even more calumnious.

At Rhodes, an enchanting place, we wondered how any one could ever have imagined that the famous bronze Colossus actually straddled across the mouth of the harbour, which is several hundred yards in width, so that sailing ships were said to have entered between his legs. Even our own Shakespeare may have shared the popular illusion when he wrote:

Why, man, he doth bestride the narrow world
Like a Colossus, and we petty men
Walk under his huge legs.

The error was more inexplicable since the shattered fragments of the Colossus, after its overthrow by an earthquake, lay for nearly nine hundred years on the ground on one side of the entrance, where it had fallen.

From Smyrna we chartered a special train to visit the Temple of Artemis at Ephesus, the patient explorer of which, Mr. Wood, I afterwards met at Constantinople.

Landing at Chanak on the Asiatic shore of the Hellespont – destined more than thirty years later to be a name of such grave portent to British arms – we investigated the sites of Bounarbashi and Hissarlik, rival claimants to the title of "Windy Troy", and had little hesitation in pronouncing in favour of Schliemann's hypothesis; although it was difficult either to imagine the relatively insignificant mound of Hissarlik, not eighty feet in height – notwithstanding that it was the site of seven superimposed cities – as once crowned with the "topless towers of Ilium", or to believe, with a later poet than Marlowe, that here,

Ilion like a mist rose into towers.

At Constantinople we saw all the sights. We visited the mosques; we attended the mid-day service at St. Sofia and gazed from a gallery at the long line of worshippers far down below, bending to and fro, bowing, kneeling, and touching the ground with their foreheads, with almost machine-like regularity, while the deep tones of the Imam rang through the vaulted spaces, and the wild and dissonant responses of the readers in the *dikkeh*, or reading pulpit, filled the dome with strange and long-drawn echoes. We saw the Dancing Dervishes at Galata, and the Howling Dervishes at Scutari (not by any means the only ones I have met), where also the prostrate forms of the worshippers, including tiny children, were walked upon by the Imam, an individual of no mean size; we rowed up the Golden Horn, and we rode round by Byzantine walls of the Old City; we attended the Selamlik and saw the cowering form of Abdul Hamid in his phaeton, fenced in with mounted guards; and of course we chaffered in the bazaars.

At Constantinople we separated, to return to England by different routes. But hereby hangs my little tale, which gives its title to this slender excerpt from a forgotten diary. The quintet who had journeyed so long and so happily together, but whose ways in life were henceforward to be so divergent, entered into a solemn pledge to meet in the East End of London at the hospitable board of one of the two clergymen on a given date in June. No engagement, however important, no counter-attraction,

We saw the Dancing Dervishes at Galata.

however great, was to induce any one of the five to abstain from the tryst. He was to suffer all the penalties of the damned if he were to fail.

On the appointed day in June four of us assembled at the luncheon-table of the cleric. But the gay American was absent; nor had any letter or telegram been received from him to explain or excuse his defalcation. We drank his health, but condemned his desertion.

Some weeks later he walked into my lodgings in London. I seized him warmly by the hand, only to elicit a long excruciating howl of pain. Then for the first time I observed that his right arm was bound to his side. Upon my inquiring what had befallen him to account for his shocking breach of trust, he replied that on that very day he had been engaged in fighting a duel, from which he had emerged the vanquished. He told me the story. From Constantinople he had drifted to Paris, where, being in a dancing-saloon with a lady partner at midnight, he had had an encounter with an insolent Frenchman, who had mistaken him for an Englishman – we were not very popular in Paris at that time – and had gratuitously picked a quarrel with him. The Frenchman had trodden deliberately upon the dress of the lady; whereupon the American squire, resenting the affront, had charged the Frenchman with having intentionally besmirched the skirts of his companion. The insolent Frenchman had replied that the dress of the lady could not be more soiled than was her character, upon which the intrepid American had at once, and very properly, knocked him down.

This was of course followed by a challenge to a duel, and my American friend, who had never held a rapier or fired a shot in anger in his life, found himself committed to this unwelcome form of encounter. The choice of arms fell to his opponent, who naturally selected the weapon with which his countrymen were most familiar. The place of combat was fixed for a spot just across the frontier in the territories either of Belgium or Luxemburg – I forget which. My friend spent the short interval in taking lessons in the *escrime*, but he had not advanced far in his studies when the fatal day arrived. His fencing master had, however, advised him to make up for any lack of science or skill by dashing in, and if possible wounding his adversary before the latter had realised the nature of the assault. This was, I believe, the plan which, some years later, enabled the worthy French Premier, M. Floquet, to get the better of that fiery Napoleon of the music-halls, General Boulanger, in the duel to which the latter had challenged him. The civilian pricked the soldier in the face before the latter knew where he was; and from that hour the fate of the adventurer may be said to have been sealed.

My American friend contemplated a similar manoeuvre. He described to me the scene in a pinewood, the measured ground, the attendant seconds, the opening formalities, his own desperate trepidation. When the signal was given he rushed in with a terrific lunge. But, as he explained to me, his next, and that an immediate sensation, was finding his opponent's weapon sticking right through his right arm between the shoulder and the elbow. The duel was over, honour was satisfied; the heroes of this idiotic drama shook hands; and my friend returned to Paris to be nursed of his wound.

Hence his failure to attend the reunion banquet in the East End of London. My poor friend must have been predestined to disaster, for he was drowned a little while later, when bathing off the Mexican coast.

The Captured Colonel

> But that I am forbid
> To tell the sucrets of my prison-house,
> I could a tale unfold.
> SHAKESPEARE., *Hamlet*, Act I. Scene IV.

WHEN I was at Cairo in the winter of 1882 I encountered an English Colonel who was for a brief period the hero or the victim of a diplomatic incident that earned him no small notoriety, and involved Her Majesty's Government in a pecuniary sacrifice which they were loth to accept. The Colonel, who was the owner of a small property near L- in Turkish territory, was seized and carried off at night by a party of Greek brigands under a famous desperado, and was held in captivity, as he told me, for a period of thirty-two days. The bandits declined to surrender their prize for any less sum than £21,000, with a number of gold watches and chains thrown in; and this ransom, which the Colonel was alone in not regarding as excessive, had to be paid by Her Majesty's Government. Indeed the chief of the band sent a message to the British Consul, who was conducting the negotiations for the release, which contained the conventional but still formidable threat: "If the ransom is not paid to the last farthing, I shall send in six days his nose, in seven days his ears, and on the eighth day his head." In these circumstances Her Majesty's Government had no alternative but to surrender. With commendable astuteness, however, they reimbursed themselves by deducting the sum from the revenues of Cyprus, which were at that time paid over to the Turkish Government.

As such, the transaction was one that gave a certain degree of satisfaction to all parties. The Colonel regained his freedom, and was, so to speak, weighed, as certain Eastern potentates are in the habit of being, against his weight in gold. The British Government extricated their representative without being really out of pocket. The Turks, although penalised, nevertheless escaped the indignity of having to make a cash payment. The brigands got the loot and the watches which they desired.

But one thing rankled in the breast of the Colonel. The latter, who was an unmarried man, professed the greatest indignation that the announcement in the Press, circulated to the four corners of Europe, had been couched in the following terms:

Le Colonel et sa femme ont été pris par les brigands.

This aspersion upon his moral character and upon the austerity of his domestic existence at L- would, he thought, greatly damage him in the eyes of the Government whom he served. He spent a good deal of time, therefore, in assuring me, as I have no doubt he had done to his official superiors, that the phrase in question was a misprint, and that what had really been sent out was the following:

Le Colonel et sa ferme ont été pris par les brigands.

The Colonel was the owner of a small property.

I believe that the Colonel was innocent. On the other hand, there was a strong party, indeed the majority, who persisted in holding, in spite of his assertions, that the printer had been maligned, and that the revised version rendered insufficient homage to the traditions and the practices of the East.

In the Bull Ring

BULLFIGHT NEWS

The Cadiz bullfight went well. The Nuñez de Prado bulls were brave and began by ridding themselves of 15 horses. Frascuelo was up to his usual tricks and Angel Pistor did well. The spectators whistled at Lagartijo and Cara-Ancha. The Benjumean bulls came off badly – despite the fact that one of them was very experienced.

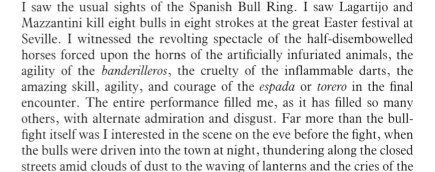

I saw the usual sights of the Spanish Bull Ring. I saw Lagartijo and Mazzantini kill eight bulls in eight strokes at the great Easter festival at Seville. I witnessed the revolting spectacle of the half-disembowelled horses forced upon the horns of the artificially infuriated animals, the agility of the *banderilleros*, the cruelty of the inflammable darts, the amazing skill, agility, and courage of the *espada* or *torero* in the final encounter. The entire performance filled me, as it has filled so many others, with alternate admiration and disgust. Far more than the bull-fight itself was I interested in the scene on the eve before the fight, when the bulls were driven into the town at night, thundering along the closed streets amid clouds of dust to the waving of lanterns and the cries of the horsemen urging them on, until they were penned in their stalls in the great amphitheatre, where they were to be shut up foodless till their ordeal of the morrow.

But the feature of the Spanish crowd that struck me most was its personal attitude, sometimes of frenzied admiration, sometimes of passionate ridicule and fury, directed at the principal actors, whether human or animal, in the drama. If one of the fighters showed skill and address, he would be frantically applauded; if he missed a series of strokes or offended against any of the rules of the game, still more if he appeared to be lacking in personal courage, he would be as unmercifully hissed, and oranges, empty bottles, old shoes and hats would be hurled at him from the crowd. Similarly, if the bull put up a good fight, he was loudly cheered. If he funked or declined to fight, he was overwhelmed with derision and contempt – poor brute – as though he had been guilty of some culpable misdemeanour. Indeed, not only was he personally abused, but his family and ancestry were held up to equal execration.

All this seemed very foreign to British ideas of sport. English crowds

I saw the usual sights of the Spanish Bull Ring.

occasionally indulge in a little "barracking" if a particularly "stonewall" bat defends his wicket without adding to the score. But I have never heard a football player hissed for missing a goal; still less a racehorse calumniated for coming in last in a race.

But the Spanish temperament in its ardour for the national sport identifies itself with the triumphs or the *láches* of man and beast alike, and, if it applauds their exploits, is equally indifferent to their failure or suffering. I can never forget one such scene of which I was a witness in the great Bull Ring of Malaga.

Just as the *espada* lunged with the sword, at the very instant that he sprang aside, the bull with a rapid twist of its lowered head was upon him. He was caught and tossed like a feather bolster into the air; he fell; in a second again he was aloft, transfixed on that terrible point. There was a vision of glittering silver spangles, violet silk breeches, and white stockings, as they were twirled round in mid-air, and then a heavy thud as the body was dashed again to the ground.

A cry of momentary horror broke even from that callous assembly. Thousands sprang excitedly from their seats; many dashed down to the arena to get a nearer view of what was happening; the personal friends of the bullfighter leaped the barricade to offer their services. The unhappy man, staggering for a moment to his feet, and striving ineffectually to combine with the physical courage that never deserted him the strength that was fast ebbing away, fell into the arms of the surrounding *matadors*. He had two gaping wounds, one in the back of the right thigh, the other in the groin – the two places where the cruel point had been driven home.

One of the doors in the barrier was opened; the procession carrying the wounded man disappeared down the gangway beyond. The excitement subsided as quickly as it had arisen; the crowd resumed their seats, and the entertainment proceeded exactly as though nothing had occurred. That evening the victim died.

Few perhaps who see the sport and applaud the skill realise the prodigious risks incurred in the final stage. The death roll of famous *toreros,* though perhaps not great in proportion to the numbers engaged, is the most eloquent comment. Of those whom I saw nearly forty years ago the most celebrated happily survived their experience of the arena. Mazzantini, who had been both a station-master and an operatic singer, ended his public career as Civil Governor of Cadiz! Lagartijo and Frascuelo became small landed proprietors, and remained popular heroes on their farms. But others, in addition to the Malaga victim, whose name I forget, were less fortunate, and lost their lives on the field of action. The most recent champion of the ring, Joselito, was killed at Talavera in 1920. The year 1922 claimed the lives of Varelito and Granero.

How I Won A Vote

Cast thy bread upon the waters: for thou shalt find it after many days.
Ecclesiastes xi. 1.

———※———

WHEN I was standing for Parliament in South Derbyshire in the General Election of 1885 – a contest in which I was handsomely beaten, but in which every vote might have been of value – my agent at Derby received a telegram from an unknown person a few days before the poll, which contained these mysterious words:

"Is the Mr. Curzon who is standing for South Derbyshire the gentleman who travelled in a first-class railway carriage from Catania to Girgendi on May 1, 1885? If so I will come and vote for him."

My agent, who had never heard either of Catania or Girgenti, brought me this cryptic message, as to the significance of which I was myself a little uncertain. It was true that in the spring of that year, after climbing Etna, I had proceeded from Catania to Girgenti by train. But I could not for the moment recall any more precise memory of the journey. Nor had I my diary with me to refresh my recollection of what might have passed.

The telegram was answered in the affirmative, and I forgot all about it, until on the polling day, happening to go into the agent's office, I found a gentleman there who acknowledged the authorship of the message and revealed his identity. Then and there I remembered an English traveller who with his wife had journeyed with me in the same compartment, and with whom I had entered into conversation. He had apparently seen my name on a label on my hat-box, and reading in the pages that a Conservative candidate of the same name was standing for South Derbyshire, for which he happened to possess a vote, and being a sound Conservative himself, he had, in receiving my agent's reply to his first inquiry, decided to come down and give me his support.

Gladly did we exchange salutations and revive the memories of that half-forgotten day. And then it was that I learned what had won the favour of my unknown friend.

"Do you not remember," he said, "that as the train wound in and out of the parched Sicilian valleys, the young man with the hat-box kept pointing to the sister heights of Castro Giovanni and Calascibetta, rearing their magnificent natural bastions crowned with the ruins of feudal towers, high into the air; how he told us that Castro Giovanni, the nobler of the two elevations, 2600 feet above the sea, was the Enna of the Ancients, where Proserpine had been carried off by Pluto; how the young man quoted Cicero, who had thus described it:

Enna est loco perexcelso atque edito, quo in summo est aequata agro planities, et aquae perennes; tota vero ab omni aditu circumcisa atque dirempta est; quam circa lacus lucique sunt plurimi et laetissimi flores omni tempore anni;

Mr. Curzon who is standing for South Derbyshire (a contest in which I was handsomely beaten).

51

(Henna is in a very lofty and elevated place on the top of which there is a smooth level plain and ever-flowing springs; but the whole place is cut off and separated from all approach; around it there are many lakes and groves, and most joyous flowers every season of the year.)

how he said that Newman in Callista had referred to its castled splendour; and how it reminded him somewhat of Acrocorinthos lifting its battlemented crest above the waters of the Gulf of Corinth; and also of the fortress Peak of Banias or Cesarea Philippi in Palestine; and how in those now desolate surroundings -- the result of surface mining – Proserpine would hardly have been tempted to stray in search of flowers, and the hunting hounds could scarcely have lost their scent (as the legend goes) for the exceeding fragrance of the surroundings? Do you not further remember," he said, "as the train twisted in and out, now showing the great summit on one side now on the other, how the young man with the hat-box kept jumping up and insisting that his fellow-passengers should share his enthusiasm, and exchange seats with him, and enjoy the spectacle?"

Later on I looked up my diary, and there indeed was the reference, and there lay the explanation of the vote so easily and gaily won; and therefrom sprang a friendship with my companion of the Sicilian railway carriage, whose vote was ever at the disposal of the Conservative candidate for South Derbyshire, doomed in the great majority of cases, I regret to say, to be not more fortunate in his electoral fortunes than the young man with the hat-box was in November 1885.

Every vote might have been of value.

SOUTH DERBYSHIRE ELECTION,
1885.

MR. CURZON
REQUESTS THE HONOUR OF YOUR
VOTE AND INTEREST.

The Billiard Table of Napoleon

IN 1908 during a compulsory stay of a fortnight at Grand Canary and the subsequent long sea voyage to St. Helena, I had made a careful study of every available work about the Emperor's residence in that island (having indeed provided myself with a miniature library for the purpose), and when I arrived at Longwood, the scene of his five years' exile and ultimate death, I was as familiar with the identity and history of every room in the building, as though I had lived in it myself.

My knowledge was soon put to an unexpected test. As I entered the house I found the French Consul, who, as representative of the French Government, was living at New Longwood (the property having been handed over by the British Government to Napoleon III, in 1858), about to conduct a party of French visitors round the building. In the entrance room, upon the walls of which hung a board inscribed "Salle d'Attente", he was expatiating upon the uses to which this apartment had been put in the time of the Emperor. "This," he said, "was the Reception Room where His Majesty received his guests." "Excuse me," said I, "this was, at any rate in the first few years of the Emperor's residence, the Billiard Room; it was always known and described as such; in it stood the billiard

Longwood, the scene of his five years' exile and ultimate death.

table on which he used to knock about the balls either with a mace or with his hands, but which, after he became tired of the game, he had removed." The Consul had never heard of the table or of the Emperor's amusement upon it; but observing that I seemed to have a greater acquaintance with the contents of the house than himself, he very courteously asked me to take the company round, which I proceeded to do, explaining with sufficient fullness the purpose to which each apartment had been put, and the furniture which it had contained. Thus I acted as guide in a house which I had never previously seen. The Consul, with much good humour, offered to vacate his post permanently in my favour.

The Billiard Room of Napoleon, which was originally built on to the house by Admiral Sir George Cockburn in 1815, when he reconstructed Longwood for the accommodation of the Emperor, is the largest room in the building, being 26 feet 6 inches long, 17 feet 6 inches broad, and 12 feet 4 inches high – and having as many as five windows. It is built of wood, and the inner walls are painted a dark green, through which in some cases could be seen the names that had been cut by earlier visitors. Here a billiard table had been placed by Sir Hudson Lowe in July 1816 for the delectation of the illustrious inmate; and here in the early days he used to play with his staff, and to knock the balls about with the young lady from the Briars (daughter of the English purveyor of Longwood), Miss Elizabeth Balcombe, afterwards Mrs. Abell, whom the Emperor used to call Mlle. Betsee and the French writers to describe as Miss Betzi. In the later editions of her vivacious work, *Recollections of the Emperor Napoleon*, which were ampler than the first, Mrs. Abell thus recalled the experiences of her youth:

He used to knock the balls about with a mace.

> Billiards was a game much played by Napoleon and his suite. I had the honour of being instructed in its mysteries by him; but when tired of my lesson, my amusement consisted in aiming the balls at his fingers, and I was never more pleased than when I succeeded in making him cry out.

And again:

> I caught sight of the Emperor in his favourite billiard room and, not being able to insist on having a game with him, I bounded off, leaving my father in dismay at the consequences likely to ensue. Instead of my anticipated game, I was requested to read a book by Dr. Warden, Surgeon of the *Northumberland*, that had just come out.

Later on, when Napoleon used this room for working, he would spread his maps and plans upon the billiard table. Finally he asked to have it removed altogether; and from that date to the time of my visit it had disappeared from view, no book about the furniture and equipment of the exile (of which there are many) having succeeded in tracing it.

Later on I went to lunch with the Governor at Plantation House, so famous as the residence of Sir Hudson Lowe. It is a very pleasant and solidly built structure of the English middle-sized country-house type, erected in the early nineteenth century, and containing some good-sized

rooms. I asked to see any furniture that might have belonged to Napoleon, and learned that the only pieces were a big English-made mahogany bookcase from Old Longwood, a mirror, and a third piece from New Longwood, which the Emperor had of course neither ever seen or used.

In an unused room, however, at the back of the house my eye fell upon an English billiard table of a rather remarkable type. It had six legs instead of eight, and its dimensions were 11 feet 4 inches by 6 feet 1 inch, and there was an inlaid pattern of ivory and some coloured wood round the edge. I asked if there was any history attached to it and was informed that there was none.

"That," I said at once, "must be the billiard table of Napoleon. How can it be any other? Would the British government ever have provided so ornamental a table for one of its own servants? When Napoleon turned out the table from the entrance room at Longwood what became of it? Manifestly it reverted to the possession of the Government. What then would Sir Hudson Lowe do with it? The obvious course was to move it to his own house, where it has remained ever since, being too big and too heavy to part with and too interesting to sell."

This chain of reasoning seemed to have a good deal to be said in its favour, until my attention was called to the disconcerting fact that there was a very fresh-looking ivory tablet on the side of the table, containing

The house where my eye fell upon an English billiard table of a rather remarkable type.

55

the well-known name of "Thurston & Co., London." Refusing to be convinced, I suggested that an explanation should be sought from that firm of their connection with what I still persisted in regarding as this historic piece of furniture.

A few months later my humble essay in inductive logic was justified; for I heard from the Governor that in 1898 the table had been thoroughly repaired, when Messrs. Thurston had supplied new cushions and pockets and had affixed their ivory mark. Further inquiry elicited that the table was no other than Napoleon's, an old inhabitant of the island, still living, having been told so by Mr. Stephen Pritchard, who was a young man in St. Helena during Napoleon's exile. The tradition, however, seems to have died out at a comparatively early date, as the table fell into a state of disrepair. Indeed, one Governor was proved to have used it at first as a carpenter's bench, and later as a screen across a door leading into the backyard!

On a closer examination the bed of the table was found to be a marvellous piece of joinery, consisting of small pieces of inch-thick oak dove-tailed together like a parquet floor (I suppose that in those days slate was either difficult to procure or was unknown). The marking board (by Fernyhough of 36 Silver Street, Gordon Square, London) still hangs in the room and is certainly the original board belonging to the table, the scoring only showing up to 21, which was the old game when people played with the mace or butt.

Such was one of the minor discoveries which my visit to St. Helena enabled me to make – perhaps I may tell elsewhere about the others. But I still remain lost in wonder at the *nepenthe* which for three-quarters of a century had drugged the successive occupants of Plantation House and their innumerable visitors into complete oblivion of so interesting a prize.

The Palaestra of Japan

Ostenditque humeros latos, alternaque iactat
Bracchia protendens, et verberat ictibus auras.
VIRGIL, *Aeneid*, v. 376.

... and displays his broad shoulders and stretching out his arms beats
each in turn and lashes the breezes with blows.

———✦———

AMONG the most fair and fanciful of cities is Kioto, the ancient seat of
the Empire and capital of Japan. For a thousand years it was the cage
whose gilded bars immured the unseen but sacred person of the Mikado.
Within the blind walls of the palace-enclosure the Royal *fainéant* dawdled
away a linnet-like existence. Outside, the bulk of his people torpidly
acquiesced in the rule, however fallible, of a son of the gods. Under the
guise of an Imperial theocracy, Japan was in reality a playground for the
military adventurer, and Kioto the focus of Court intrigue. A heavy
curtain of mystery, the joint weaving of the palace and the priesthood,
enveloped the sacred pile, and hermetically concealed it from alien eyes.
It was only in the latter part of the last decade that the folds were torn
asunder, and that Kioto became accessible to foreigners. The Mikado
and his Court were moved to Tokio; the Castle was dismantled; the
temple doors were thrown open, and the traveller was at liberty to
ransack shrines and secret places and sanctuaries with inquisitive
impunity.

The town is exquisitely situated in a cup between mountain ranges,
quaintly outlined, and clothed with an astonishing wealth of trees. From
the eastern range, where the visitor is probably lodged, he will get a
wonderful outlook, both at sunrise and at nightfall. In the early dawn the
entire city is drowned in a sea of white vapour, from which only the huge
hooded roofs of the temples emerge, black and solemn, like the inverted
hulls of gigantic ships. Suddenly, across the mist booms the sonorous
stroke of some vast temple-bell, and rolls away in melancholy vibrations.
At night the dusky mass of houses, stretching for miles, twinkles with the
light of a thousand lanterns that glimmer from the lintels and dance along
the streets. A swarm of fire-flies would seem to be flitting in the aisles of
some dim and sombre forest, from whose recesses float upwards the
indescribable hum of congregated humanity, street cries and laughter,
the sound of voices, and the tinkling of guitars.

At festival time, and when the *matsuris*, or religious holidays, are
celebrated, Kioto is especially worthy of a visit. The whole town turns out
merry-making; the temple precincts are blocked from morn till night by
gaily-dressed crowds; the tea-houses overflow with customers; the
singing girls extract rich harvest; and copper pieces rain into the tills of
itinerant purveyors of entertainment and theatrical shows. One street in
particular is ablaze with a succession of gaudily-decorated booths, con-

taining acrobats, jugglers, story-tellers, peep-shows, pantomimes, and plays. These are crowded from daybreak to sunset, and a forest of clogs and sandals, suspended on the outer wall, testified to the thronged condition of the pit within. In the dried-up bed of the river which intersects the town, and which at different periods presents the opposite appearance of a gutter and a torrent, will probably be erected a gigantic booth, surrounded with gaudy bannerets flying from lofty poles. A stream of passengers pouring into the entrance shows that some exhibition of interest and popularity is being enacted within. It was in the wake of such a crowd, and on such an occasion, that, at Kioto, I first made acquaintance with the *palaestra* of Japan.

We do not require the authority of the bas-reliefs of Thebes and Nineveh, or even of the 32nd chapter of Genesis, to learn that wrestling must have been one of the earliest methods of conflict in vogue among ancient peoples. The light of nature must have very soon suggested this mode of encounter between human beings. Weapons may not always have been forthcoming. A duel of blows, *i.e.* a boxing match, would involve the victory of the more practised. Whenever two combatants were engaged in a personal struggle, it would be the spontaneous instinct of the one who was placed at a disadvantage, either of implements or of skill, to close with his adversary, and submit to the practical test of bodily agility or strength. In this way would he be most likely to equalise the handicap of fists, or club, or sword. But here, again, there would be an inequality of conditions in favour of the stronger muscles and more seasoned strength, to redress which the study and science of wrestling would come into being. Hence it is not surprising to find that, among the peoples of whose remote history records are preserved, wrestling seems to have been early reduced to a system and practised as an art.

We are perhaps best acquainted with the types of wrestling in use among the ancient Greeks, and among our own countrymen in the extreme north and west of England; familiar to us, in the one case, from the illustrations on vases and sculptures, in the other from the yearly exhibitions of the craft that are given in London. African travellers have also written curious accounts of the art as practised among negro tribes. To all these systems Japanese wrestling offers certain points of resemblance, but to none more closely (though with notable points of divergence) than to the ancient Homeric fashion, as described in the famous contest between Ajax and Ulysses in the twenty-third book of the *Iliad*. The early manner of Greek wrestling was as widely distinct from the later, from the trial of skill described by Plutarch, as was a crossbow from a Martini-Henry rifle; and among the many evidences of primitive habit and ancient date supplied by the Homeric poems, the story of the wrestling match might be quoted as a not insignificant item. The art was manifestly as yet in its infancy; there was an ingenuous laxity of rule; the performance was a rough-and-tumble one at the best; and if Ajax and Ulysses had depended for fame on their feats in the *palaestra*, the reputation of neither would have long survived. In Japan, a country combining a feverish proficiency in many of the habits of advanced civilisation with uncompromising relics of feudal crystallisation, we observe a similar innocence of science, and adhesion to archaic tradition, in the ways of the wrestling ring.

On the day that I speak of, at Kioto, the contest announced was between the combined representatives of that city and the neighbouring town of Osaka, and the champions of the modern capital, Tokio. The latter, in spite of the double recruiting ground of their adversaries, achieved an easy victory – a result which was received with extreme despondency by the local partisans, but was fortunately unattended by the scenes of violence that occurred on a famous occasion of a very similar character in our own history, when, on Lammas Day, 1223, the wrestlers of London having paid a visit to those of Westminster, and gained a victory at their expense, the bailiff of Westminster and his myrmidons, whose patriotism was incensed at the local discomfiture, picked a quarrel with the triumphant Londoners, and drove them back with slaughter into the precincts of the city. No such savage reprisals followed the collapse of the heroes of Kioto and Osaka on this occasion. Only a reproachful silence overhung the piqued and disgusted crowd.

I must here explain that I am not now writing about *Jiu-Jitsu*, the more familiar form of Japanese exercise or wrestling, which is taught as the art of self-defence, but about *Sumo*, the ancient, traditional, popular, semi-scientific, semi-religious wrestling of Japan; *Sumo* with its professional schools in that country, its forty-eight chief devices (each with eight variations), its guild of carefully-trained, intensively fed, obese practitioners, its ritual, half-serious and half-comic, its still unshaken hold, corresponding to the vogue of football in England, upon the populace in Japan. Twelve years ago, long after my Kioto experiences, a troupe of forty of the more eminent professors of this art came to England and gave a series of performances at the Japan-British exhibition at Shepherd's Bush. I saw them there as I had seen their compatriots twenty years earlier in Japan: and the existence and methods of this school struck me on both occasions as one of the most curious survivals in that country, where the traditional and the up-to-date are so strangely interwoven.

In 1863 Sir Rutherford Alcock wrote:

Monmouth courted popularity by occasionally indulging in a bout.

Wrestling is to the Japanese what the ring is to us and something specially national. Every prince has a whole group of wrestlers, and their pride is to have the biggest, heaviest, and fattest; so that they generally look bloated, overfed, and disgusting as prize oxen for the butcher at Christmas. I am at a loss to understand how such men of flesh and fat can put on any great strength – they grapple very fiercely but seldom seem to throw each other.

Since those days Japanese wrestling has experienced much the same transition as overtook its counterpart, once practised by kings and nobles in England (Henry VIII was quite a good wrestler, and a century and a half later Monmouth courted popularity by occasionally indulging in a bout in rustic sports) when in the growing disrepute of Feudalism, it passed from the mansions of the great to the village green and the fairs and festivals of the people. Similarly in Japan, when the old order was broken up by the Revolution, and the castles, retinues, and princely maintenance of the nobility became a thing of the past, wrestling lost its hold upon the titled classes and became the sport of the crowd. But even so, it retains a quasi-hieratic prestige, because of its connection with the celebrated Ekoin Temple at Tokio, the strict etiquette and observances of the guild, and the popularity attaching to its principal practitioners, who are regarded in Japan with almost as much reverence as a great bull-fighter at Seville or Madrid.

To an outsider, unversed in the esoteric rules of the art, the performance is apt to appear more comic than serious – and I found the greatest difficulty in believing, either in Japan or London, that the scene which I witnessed had a scientific or a symbolic importance. But I will endeavour to be fair by giving the latter wherever I can.

The scene of action at Kioto was the booth in the dried-up river bed to which I referred. It was built and roofed with wattled bamboos, between whose interstices the air entered and made a pleasing temperature. The interior accommodated several hundred persons, mainly squatted on the ground, though a small, raised platform, divided into compartments, ran round the wall, for the accommodation of wealthier or more luxurious patrons. Every eye was directed at a raised structure in the centre, rectangular in shape, and about 18 feet square, constructed of bags of sand, packed one upon the other to a height of about 3 feet above the floor. At the four corners of the parallelogram were tall poles reaching to the roof, with gaudily-coloured flags, inscribed with native characters, depending between them at the top. This dais is said to have been a four-columned temple in its origin and still to retain a symbolic significance. In its centre a circle, about 12 feet in diameter, was marked out by a plaited belt of straw, worked into the soil, and was strewn with smooth yellow sand. This was the arena in which the combatants were about to engage, and out of which one of the two must hurl or thrust or throw his adversary before he could claim the victory.

A third person was also admitted on to the raised artificial platform. This was the umpire, a grotesque sworded figure, clad in a reproduction of the old court costume of Japan, with projecting skirts, and a stiff excrescence standing out like wings on either side of his back, and flapping as he moved. Carrying in his hand, as an emblem of his office, a species of lacquered fan, which at critical moments he fluttered furiously, he took his stand just outside the magic circle, recited to the audience in a prolonged shriek the names of the combatants, placed them in position, and then went off into an unintelligible gabble of sound, growing louder and louder, and quicker and quicker, till the wrestlers had closed, when his ejaculations culminated in a succession of screams, while he danced about the platform like a maniac, to get a fair view of the contest, to decide the points, and to adjudicate upon fair play.

And now as to the combatants themselves, the Milos of Tokio and Osaka, the pets of the national *palaestra*. Though for days I had seen their

A pair of huge and burly figures, veritable Goliaths of Gath.

The distinguishing feature of the Japanese contest seemed to be that nothing was unfair.

photographs being hawked about the streets, I must confess I was staggered when I set eyes upon the living originals. As their names were called out, from opposite sides there advanced on to the arena a pair of huge and burly figures, veritable Goliaths of Gath, marvels of flesh whatever they might be of muscle, tall in stature, big of girth, and elephantine in proportions – a wholly different type of animal from the average Japanese, who is a squat little fellow, nimble as a monkey, and less than 5 feet in height. Some of the wrestlers were men of medium height, but the majority were of extravagant size and dimensions, and appeared to belong to a distinct species, the peculiar attributes of which had been transmitted by a careful manipulation of the stock from one generation to another. They wore their hair in the old Japanese fashion, now rapidly falling into desuetude, with a stiffly-greased top-knot brought forward and laid horizontally upon the crown. Their features were not conspicuous for refinement, and wore an expression of intolerable swagger. Their bodies were plentifully embellished with small circular patches of sticking-plaster, concealing artificial burns – a prescription very popular in the Japanese pharmacopoeia as a counter-irritant to any pain or malady that may happen to be in existence – or with the cicatrices which similar patches had once covered, and rows of which extended symmetrically down their brawny backs. Like the Homeric wrestlers, they were naked save for a $\pi\epsilon\rho\iota\zeta\omega\mu\alpha$ or girdle – in this case a broad tasselled belt of dark blue silk, passing between the legs and round the loins, and fitting so tightly to the figure that the antagonist could with difficulty squeeze his fingers in to get a grip.

The rival competitors having stepped on to the arena, I naturally anticipated that they would soon fall to. Such expectations were based on a most mistaken estimate of the elasticity of the Japanese code, in which preliminaries, if importance be measured by time, transcend at least tenfold the trial of strength itself. These preliminaries may be divided into two parts: self-advertisement on the part of each individual champion, and co-operate bravado by the pair before the real bout begins. Either wrestler first advances with great solemnity to the edge of the platform, and faces the crowd. Lifting his right leg high in the air, and extending it as far as possible from the body, he brings it down on the ground with a vigorous stamp, at the same time that he also brings down his right hand with a resounding smack upon his right thigh. Then up goes the left leg, and along with it the left hand, and down come both with a thud at a similar angle on the left side; which done, and having strained and tested his sinews by this remarkable manoeuvre, the wrestler straightens himself and gazes proudly around at the gaping audience. Then he lounges to a corner of the platform, sips a mouthful of water from a small wooden pail, and squirts it through his lips over his arm and chest and legs. Next, a paper napkin is handed to him by an attendant, with which he carefully wipes his face and body. Finally, from a little wooden box affixed to the corner-pole, he takes a pinch of salt between his fingers, and tosses it into the air for luck. This act I was told had also a moral significance, as indicating a complete absence of ill-will between the combatants, while the pundits further ascribe to it some unexplained sacrificial value. These precautions satisfactorily completed, the champion probably goes through the stretching and stamping performance once again, until at last he is ready to play his part in the serio-comedy that then ensues.

Both athletes now take up their positions on opposite sides of the ring, and, squatting down upon their haunches, *vis-à-vis*, stretch out their arms and gently rub together the palms of their hands, which they then open outwards with a gesture of magnificent civility. Having satisfied this formality, which appears to correspond to the handshake of two English pugilists, they retire once more to their respective corners and repeat the performance with water, paper napkin, and salt. Some seven or eight minutes must have been consumed in these formalities, and patience is well-nigh exhausted, when at length they proceed into the middle of the ring, and again squat down like two monstrous baboons, exactly opposite each other, and with their foreheads all but touching.

The judge now plants himself on one side, brandishes his fan, and commences the series of mystic ejaculations before alluded to. While his jabber waxes fiercer and fiercer, they are seen to rise slightly from the crouching attitude, and to face each other with alert eyes and out-stretched arms, ready to grip or to rush in. But not yet is the visitor sure of his money's worth; for even at this advanced juncture one or other of the antagonists will casually loaf out of the ring, stroll back to his corner, and resume the water and salt masquerade – a gratification for which he finds all the readier excuse if, as frequently happens, one of the two parties has seized an unfair advantage in grappling, and the umpire has called "False Start". A similar plea, too, may justify the interpolation of a fresh scene in the comedy, such as the rubbing of a little sand under the armpits, or a seizing of the corner-pole with both hands, and straining against it with full strength. When I asked any of my neighbours what they thought of this by-play, they grinned and said, "It is Japanese fashion"; with which simple effort of ratiocination their minds appeared to be quite content.

At length, however – after all these struttings and stridings, these rinsings and rubbings, and feints and fiascoes – our Daniel Lamberts are once more in the ring. What happens when they are at length engaged?

Now, wrestling may be described as consisting of three varieties: that in which the object is to defeat the adversary by any means whatever, without much consideration for fair or foul; that which, while enjoying a generous latitude, is yet subjected to certain recognised prohibitions and disqualifications; and that, every phase and move of which is regulated, partly by written laws, partly by unwritten etiquette. Of the last named, the system in vogue in Cumberland and Westmorland – which is the most scientific in existence – is the best illustration; the Devon and Cornish system is a fair type of the second; while of the first or most primitive we find samples in times and countries as remote as among the Greeks of Homer, in certain parts of Lancashire at the present day, and in the palaestra of Japan.

The object of the Japanese wrestler is to force his opponent to touch the

ground with any part of his body other than his feet, or to eject him altogether from the magic circle, designated by the margin of plaited straw. It does not seem to matter much how he does this, whether by dint of superior weight, or strength, or agility, or by means of pushing, or tugging, or lifting, or throwing. He may hit his antagonist with his fist or even seize him by the hair. Sometimes the struggle is the work of a few seconds; sometimes it is prolonged for minutes. As a rule, the men seem most averse to grappling; or if by chance they have succeeded in closing, instead of aiming at a firm and fair grip, they will encircle each other's shoulders or body with one hand, while with the other they make frantic efforts to grab hold of the tight waistband of the adversary, in order to secure a more reliable purchase. Thus their energy is consumed in the double effort to wriggle out of reach themselves, and yet to catch hold of their antagonist. Sometimes the more powerful man, like Ajax, in the 23rd Book of the *Iliad*, will lift his opponent clean off the ground. Sometimes, too, the latter, like Ulysses, will reverse the advantage by the exercise of cunning. Sometimes, like the two Homeric heroes, they sprawl side by side. Occasionally the contest degenerates into a butting and thrusting match, as though between a pair of gigantic rams. But very rarely is any real danger incurred, or damage done, and a spectator might attend the Japanese ring for a lifetime and never witness such a scene as is described in "The Lady of the Lake", where Scott demonstrates the prowess of Lord James Douglas in the wrestling match by thus describing the condition of his vanquished opponents:

> For life is Hugh of Larbert lame,
> Scarce better John of Alloa's fame,
> Whom senseless home his comrades bare.

The distinguishing feature of the Japanese contest seemed to be that nothing was unfair; any movement was permissible; no part of the body was forbidden. One result of this is very much to shorten the struggle. As a rule, it was over in a very few moments, or at most in a few minutes – a ridiculous contrast to the exorbitant time consumed in preliminaries. One of the two combatants was thrust or pitched or rolled or tumbled out of the ring. He picked himself up and retired on the one side; the victor stepped down on the other; the audience applauded and another pair came on.

The performance at Kioto, which, after a repetition of much the same incidents scores of times in succession, became somewhat monotonous, was relieved by two episodes of a more exaggerated, though unconscious, absurdity than anything by which they had been preceded. In an interval between two stages of the competition there advanced on to the platform, one after the other, two prodigiously fat boys. I say boys, though, had I not been told that their ages were only sixteen and seventeen, I should never have guessed that these mountains of flesh, with cheeks like footballs, bellies like hogsheads, and legs like an elephant's, were anything but mature and overfed men. They wore the same scanty costume as the wrestlers, with the addition of a long and gorgeously embroidered

Among the most fair and fanciful of cities is Kioto.

65

satin apron, which depended from below their paunches to the ground. One of the pair, I was told, was the son of a distinguished wrestler; and if he might be taken to represent a smaller edition of his parent, he certainly spoke volumes for the probable proportions of the sire. I expected that these two youthful prodigies would at least give some exhibition of agility or brute strength. But not a bit. They were far too tender to wrestle, and were merely intended for parade. Each in turn went through the solemn dumb show before described. They extended and brought down with a stamp their puffy legs; they smacked their hands upon their corpulent thighs; they spread out their clumsy arms and protruded their rotund paunches; they gazed around with an air of ineffable complacency; and then they strutted off the ring with as much composure as they had marched on.

The other episode was a wrestling match between the grown-up counterparts of these Gargantuan boys; in other words, between two monsters whose appearance suggested that of fattened bulls at a Christmas show. They were clearly the idols of the ring, and were received with immense plaudits. Great flaps of superfluous fat hung about the body of the larger, and his stomach stood out like an inflated balloon. His rival was scarcely his inferior in size or ugliness. No part of the formula was omitted by these Titans. They raised and planted their unwieldy legs; they spanked their massive thighs; they squatted and drank water, and sprinkled salt, and rubbed their shining skins with the paper napkins. Finally, like two hippopotami, they collided. There was a sort of convulsive thrusting and heaving; a quaking and yielding of vast surfaces of flesh; a sound of crumbling and collapse; and then, all in a moment, the fatter of the two fat men, whose science was not on a par with his suet, rolled off the platform like a beer-barrel, and tumbled down with a crash into the crowd.

In the second bout he was bent upon revenge. His tactics were simple but efficacious. When his opponent rushed in to grapple, he stood still like a mountain, and the smaller man, crushed by sheer *avoirdupois*, rebounded off him, and subsided in a heap upon the floor.

I afterwards inquired how it was that this strange and abnormal type of manhood was produced, and I learned that it was by the practice of eugenics *in excelsis*. The wrestlers are selected in boyhood from the progeny of parents of unusual size: they are dieted and treated from the earliest years: as they grow up and enter the ring they are attended by a special bodyguard of masseurs, trainers, barbers, clothiers and cooks; they are encouraged to consume an incredible amount of strength-producing food; and they constitute a separate guild, graded, numbered, and registered according to their capacity. How a selected body of Japanese champions would fare against our North Country or West Country wrestlers I cannot conjecture. For sheer weight no Englishman could compete with these fleshy prodigies. But I expect that he would give them a good deal of active exercise to which they are unaccustomed: and I should be prepared to wager a reasonable sum as to which would first find himself "on the mat"

The "Kowtow"

At her feet he bowed, he fell, he lay down. – Judges v.27.
    He struck nine times the ground with his forehead to adore in prayer or thanksgiving the mercy of the Great Khan. – GIBBON, *Decline and Fall of the Roman Empire*, cap. lxiv.

WHEN I was in Peking in 1892, and afterwards when I wrote my book, *Problems of the Far East*, I made a special study of the history of the *kowtow*, that form of obeisance that had figured so largely in the diplomatic struggle between Europe and China for two centuries, and the final abandonment of which signified the latter's defeat. The performer of the *kowtow* kneels thrice on the ground, and on each occasion knocks his forehead three times on the floor, in sign of subjection to the Sovereign. From one point of view it may be said to mark the extremity of deference, from another the maximum of humiliation. This obeisance has figured from time immemorial as the Court ceremonial of Eastern kings; 2300 years ago the liberty-loving Athenians condemned their envoy Timagoras to death because he had *kowtowed* at Susa to Artaxerxes Mnemon, the great king. But the particular form of prostration which consists of nine blows of the forehead on the ground was consecrated by long usage to the Court of the Son of Heaven. As early as A.D. 713 an Arab Embassy from Kutaiba to the Emperor Hwen Tsang declined to perform the *kowtow* and were sentenced to death by the indignant Chinese. In the seventeenth and eighteenth centuries the Jesuit Fathers *kowtowed* without any compunction – so did the earlier European envoys to China from Holland, Russia, and Portugal. The Chinese always maintained that the first English Plenipotentiary to be admitted to an audience with the Chinese Emperor, viz. Lord Macartney, in 1793, had *kowtowed* to Kien Lung; but he declared that though he had offered to do so, if a Chinese official of equal rank would do the same to a picture of George III, with which he had provided himself, he had ended by only kneeling on one knee.

The next British Envoy, Lord Amherst, in 1816 escaped the *kowtow* because, owing to a violent dispute upon his arrival at Peking, he never saw the Emperor at all. It was in the China War of 1860 that the incident occurred which Sir France Doyle made the subject of his little poem – already a classic – entitled "The Private of the Buffs". A note prefixed to the poem explained that, some Sikhs and an English private soldier having fallen into the hands of the Chinese and been commanded to perform the *kowtow*, while the Sikhs obeyed, the English soldier declared that he would not prostrate himself before any Chinaman alive, whereupon he was immediately knocked upon the head and killed:

Yes, honour calls! – with strength like steel
    He put the vision by,
Let dusky Indians whine and kneel;

An English lad must die.
And thus, with eyes that would not shrink,
   With knee to man unbent,
Unfaltering on its dreadful brink,
   To his red grave he went.

The war was sufficient. It rang the death-knell of the *kowtow*. After the war of 1860 the *kowtow*, without being expressly mentioned in the Treaty that followed, was abolished by it for foreign representatives; and from the first ensuing audience in June 1873 to the present date it has never been either demanded or performed.

I little thought that I should ever see, much less receive, the *kowtow* myself. But in December 1901 I paid a visit to the Northern Shan States in the extreme north-easterly corner of Burma, where it touches the Chinese frontier; and there, at Lashio, I held a Durbar to receive the Sawbwas and Myozas of those distant principalities, which are not among the least loyal of the minor feudatories of the British Crown.

The ceremony was held in a thatched *pandal* or open hall, erected for the occasion and gaily adorned with bunting and gold umbrellas. I was taken to it mounted on a white pony and shaded by eight white umbrellas of state – described to me as the regulation number for the representative of a Sovereign. It was a very picturesque scene as the chiefs in their native finery came forward, one after the other, and offered their homage.

I paid a visit in the extreme north-easterly corner of Burma, where it touches the Chinese frontier.

Some years before, when Under-Secretary to Lord Salisbury in the Foreign Office in London, I had had something to do with this remote region; and I recalled the desire of a Chinese chief of a small border state, called Kokang, to be allowed to come under British jurisdiction rather than be left on the Chinese side of the boundary, which we were engaged in demarcating at that time. After the Shan chiefs had been presented, I noted in the assembly at Lashio the tall and erect figure of an elderly Chinaman dressed in the dark-blue silk robe of a mandarin, with the embroidered dragon plastron on his breast and the Chinese red-tasselled skull-cap upon his head. Below the coat he wore loose trousers of a brighter hue and long, embroidered felt-soled boots. He came forward in his turn, advanced on the carpet in front of the dais on which I was seated, bowed three times, lifting his hands high to his forehead, and dropping them again; and then and there, of his own accord, without warning, solemnly and with infinite dignity, knelt down, and three times struck his forehead on the ground. Then he rose, amid a breathless silence, repeated the salute, knelt again, and three times renewed the same obeisance. A third time he repeated the rising and the prostration, and then with imperturbable gravity rose and backed slowly down the stairs of the platform. It was my old friend of Foreign Office days, the Heng or Chief of Kokang; and the performance was all the more remarkable in that he was nearly blind, having all but lost his eyesight some time before, while making gunpowder.

The Curiosity of Li Hung Chang

There are some things which men confess with ease, and others with difficulty.
EPICTETUS, "On Inconsistency", cap. xxi.

TRAVELLERS in the East will be very familiar with one aspect of Oriental mentality, which is always amusing and often of value, if at times a little disconcerting. I allude to the idiosyncracy which prompts the Eastern, even of the highest rank, to put and to answer, with equal good manners, and with a total lack of impertinence, the most searching and intimate questions as to age, profession, family history and income.

As a rule in the West you do not, on the first occasion that you meet a stranger, ask him how old he is, whether he is married, and if so how long he has borne the yoke, what is the size of his family, and what are the emoluments of his profession. There is a certain reserve about such matters, the discussion or disclosure of which is supposed to be the reward of intimacy and to mark the later rather than the opening stages of acquaintance. But the Eastern thinks and acts quite otherwise. He wants to know what manner of person he is encountering, and to place him fairly and squarely in his normal environment. For this purpose, it is important to learn the details of his domestic existence, when he entered the world, what he has done since, what are his present circumstances, and so forth.

The Oriental is much more concerned to ascertain these elemental conditions than he is to exchange opinions or to analyse character. He is not bad at the latter operation either, but it must come in its proper place. Thus in all my travels, whether I was the guest of an Asiatic monarch, or a Kurdish chieftain, or a Persian satrap (though in the latter case the curiosity was apt to be veiled by an almost Gallic polish of manner), I was always prepared to be put through my paces in this respect, and to reveal the fullest details of my age and circumstances. I have related elsewhere how much I fell in the estimation of the Foreign Minister of Korea, when he learned that, though an ex-Minister, I was not married to a member of the British royal family!

Salary I found to be a perennial source of interest. The Eastern Governor – who lives as a rule by successful spoliation of his subjects or subordinates, and who regards office not as the gratification of an honourable ambition, but as the opportunity of replenishing a depleted exchequer – always wanted to know what an English Minister or ruler received or did in analogous conditions. What was his actual stipend? What were his perquisites? Was office a convenient and agreeable source of wealth? What powers did it enable the occupant to exercise? And did he wield them, as was fit and proper, for his own personal advantage?

Furthermore, family details never failed to interest and enthuse. Exactly how old was the visitor? How had he spent his life? How had he

I was always prepared to be put through my paces.

fared in the marriage lottery? How many children had he? What was he doing with them or they with him? I ended by feeling not the smallest resentment, but on the contrary a good deal of mild pleasure, in communicating these details – which seemed to place one on a footing of easy familiarity with the interlocutor – and I developed a laudable aptitude in putting the most penetrating questions in reply. Nor can I recall an occasion on which any of these questions either on one side or the other excited the smallest resentment, while they frequently resulted in the exchange of useful and diverting information.

I think, however, that among my hardiest interrogators I must give the palm to the famous Chinese statesman, Li Hung Chang. When I visited Tientsin in 1892, he was Viceroy of Chihli, and was already in somewhat advanced years, being over seventy-one years of age. Nevertheless at our interviews in his official *yamen* he interrogated me with a pertinacity which excited my warmest admiration; and I recall his long lean figure (he was over six feet high) clad in a grey silken robe with black silk cape, his little beady eyes, his quizzical look, and the imperturbable gravity with which he put to me the most searching questions.

A few years later he came to England, when I was Under-Secretary in the Foreign Office to Lord Salisbury, and it became my duty to conduct him to the House of Commons, which provided ample material for his rather mordant curiosity, and also to Hatfield for a garden-party. It was on the latter occasion that he achieved what I regarded as the greatest triumph in the particular line of inquiry of which I am here writing.

While we were being photographed on the terrace, he suddenly asked me once again how old I was; and upon my replying that I was thirty-six – "Dear me," he said, "you are exactly the same age as the German Emperor." I acknowledged the impeachment, whereupon he continued as follows:

Li Hung Chang: "The German Emperor, however, has six sons. How many have you?"

Curzon: "I have only recently been married, and I regret that so far I have none."

Li Hung Chang: "Then what have you been doing all this time?"

To this question I admit that I could not find, nor even now can I suggest, an appropriate answer.

OVERLEAF
It became my duty to conduct him to the House of Commons, which provided ample material for his rather mordant curiosity, and also to Hatfield for a garden-party.

On the Nile

Push off, and [standing] well in order smite
  The sounding furrows.

                         TENNYSON, *Ulysses.*

And all the way, to guide their chime,
With falling oars they kept the time.

                    A. MARVELL, *Bermudas.*

THE noise comes in violent shocks of sound across the still levels of the river. A big *Dahabeah* is being propelled by the standing rowers up the stream. In two lines abreast they stand to work the huge oars and with each jerk they repeat the cry. They are standing on inclined planks, and they take three or four steps forward as they dip the long sweeps into the water, and the same number backwards as they pull through the stroke. Both movements are made to the accompaniment of a chorus chanted in unison by the crew in response to, or in repetition of a note given by the κελευστής, who is often himself one of their number. They do not, like the ancient Greeks, time the rowing by the κέλευσμα. There is little of music and not much of rhythm in the performance. They shout the loudest when the strain is hardest; and the singing is meant not to mark the time so much as to excite and inspirit the rowers.

Presently another great *dahabeah* surges into view. It catches up the leader and they begin to race. The rival crews run forwards and backwards on the sloping planks with redoubled ardour; the air is rent with their vociferous cries; the perspiration rolls from the brows and shines on the polished skins of the straining men; and the two boats leap forward like greyhounds through the water. With a mighty effort the victory is won by one of the two competitors. As it forges ahead the shouting suddenly dies down; hoarse laughter peals across the river surface: and presently we hear only the measured dip of the two sets of oars, the victors and the vanquished, as they plunge and replunge in the silent stream.

They shout the loudest when the strain is hardest.

On the Hellespont

The light that never was on sea or land,
The consecration and the poet's dream.
WORDSWORTH, *Elegiac Stanzas*.

Now fades the glimmering landscape on the sight,
And all the air a solemn stillness holds.
T. GRAY, *Elegy in a Country Churchyard*.

———————◦❈◦———————

AFTER exploring the ruins of Troy, we had visited the tumuli of Achilles
and Patroclus, which were probably not tombs at all. We had halted at
the tumulus of Ajax, to which, if this indeed be the site, Homer directly
refers. Our route lay through the village of Ophrynium to Erenkeui. It
was nearly half an hour before sundown. The waters of the Aegean and
the Hellespont shone like aluminium in the lustrous setting of sky and
sea.

Out to the west, across the smooth and glimmering surface, a golden
haze appeared to swim between the furthermost sea-line and the heavens,
when suddenly, from this diaphanous belt of mist and light combined, a
conical shape detached itself and soared into the air. By slow degrees, as
the sky became more richly illumined by the dying light, and as the pink
flush overspread and tinged the waters, the outline gained in sharpness,
in clearness, in beauty. The shadowy pyramid was transformed into a
vast and shining form; a girdle of amethysts encircled its waist; the breath
of beauty fanned its radiant shoulders; its head was crowned with a
diadem of rubies and pearls. It was the marble peak of Athos peering
across a hundred miles of ocean.

Not for long did the fairy vision last. Presently, as the light waned, the
mountain lost its shape, its sides became blurred and were merged in
spectral vapours; the lilac changed to lavender, and the lavender faded to
grey; the crimson became red, the red became rose, and the rose turned
ashen-pale. Faint and yet fainter the outline dwindled until it was
swallowed up in the creeping shadows, and finally disappeared altogether from view. Where but a few minutes before had been the magic
of the rainbow and a glory as from the opened doors of heaven, a pall
seemed to have been let down by invisible ropes from the firmament, and
a dim and soundless quietude enveloped the scene.

I saw how all the trembling ages past,
Moulded to her by deep and deeper breath,
Neared to the hour when Beauty breathes her last,
And knows herself in death!

By the Waters of Babylon

The sun's rim dips, the stars rush out,
At one stride comes the dark.
S. T. COLERIDGE, *The Ancient Mariner.*

ONCE more I am camped on the banks of the Euphrates. The river rolls its dirty volume by. It is the late afternoon. There occurs that wonderful interlude before sundown – a time half of mystery, half of sadness – when the day passes through its death-throes and prepares for dissolution. In the tranquil radiance the riverside villages are redeemed from the filth and squalor of the day, and assume a fleeting beauty that has in it something of the divine. A bluish vapour rises from the broad river-bosom and swathes the banks with filmy kerchief. The pitchy hulls of the big one-masted boats, moored along the shore, tremble inverted in the glassy current. A rosy pink strikes redly on mud wall and mouldering rampart, and high above the flat house-tops the columnar stems and quivering plumes of a hundred palms are pencilled against the sky. Bands of saffron fringed with green, and of turquoise blending into pink, are stretched like scarves round the horizon, except where in the west the sinking orb turns half the heaven into a forge of fire. In the distance is heard the creaking of the pulleys as the oxen draw the last skins of water from the muddy wells. Nearer, the mingled sounds of human and animal life, the barking of dogs and braying of donkeys, the shrill clamour of children, the raucous ejaculations of the Asiatic mule-driver, and the eternal hubbub of the bazaar, ring out a strange but not unmusical chorus. From the village mosque tower a brazen-lunged Seyid, with fingers pressed against his ears, intones the evening prayer. And so, as the suave pomp of the Eastern sunset wanes, river and village and people and the glowing sun itself sink slowly to rest; the enchantment seems coldly to fade out and expire; an undulating vapour curls upward from the river-bed; and presently the same grey misty monochrome has enveloped all alike with its fleecy mantle. The day is dead.

Greece in the 'Eighties

Where each old poetic mountain
Inspiration breathed around,
Every shade and hallowed fountain
Murmured deep a solemn sound.
T. GRAY, *The Progress of Poesy.*

—————◦⟨❈⟩◦—————

FORTY-THREE years ago four English travellers rode through the hills
and valleys of inland Greece. All were fresh from the University or the
College. One was a Senior Classic and a future Bishop. The second was a
future Headmaster of Haileybury and Eton. The third was an Eton
Master and future Vice-Provost of the College. The fourth was a young
Oxford Graduate who had just taken his degree. Their names were J. E.
C. Welldon, Edward Lyttelton, F. E. Cornish, and G. N. Curzon.

I suppose that we had much the same experience as other travellers
who toured through Greece in that time, with perhaps two differences;
first, that Edward Lyttelton was discovered to be the nephew of Mr.
Gladstone, and that our trip in consequence became a sort of triumphal
progress, as I shall presently relate; and secondly, that the Greece we
were exploring was not in our eyes the Greece of King George, though he
was at that time on its throne, so much as it was the Greece of Homer and
Herodotus, of Pericles and Phidias, of Aeschylus and Sophocles, of
Aristotle and Plato. Thucydides and not Baedeker was our guide; we
opened our Sophocles a dozen times for every once that we glanced at
Mahaffy. When we drove to Marathon we plotted out every detail of the
battle that had been fought out years earlier, but we did not trouble much
about the poor Englishmen who had been captured (and in one case
murdered) by Greek brigands on this very road only twelve years before.
When we went down to Salamis, we spent an hour in disputing on which
"rocky brow" was placed the throne of Xerxes. When we climbed
Acrocorinthos, we found a greater magic in the fountain of Pirene,
where, if I remember rightly, Bellerophon seized Pegasus as he was
quenching his thirst, than we did in the view of the Corinth Canal.

Pericles was our companion on the Acropolis and the Areopagus even
more than Paul, and after Paul no one seemed to matter. We were never
more thrilled than when, after leaving Arakhova we came to the famous
σχιστὴ ὁδός, that fork in the hill road where Laius in his chariot met his
death at the hand of his unknown and unknowing son.

At Athens we were fortunate in meeting a number of distinguished
persons. M. Tricoupis, the Prime Minister, struck us as a capable and
patriotic statesman and was certainly a most attractive man. Dr
Schliemann, who had made a fortune at Nijni-Novgorod in tea and
indigo, and was reputed to be worth £10,000 a year, was living with his
young Greek wife in a fine house which he had built and entitled
τὸ Ἰλίου Μέγαρον, where he had a butler called Rhadamanthus. He was

himself a short, uneasy-eyed, ugly little man, his hair shaven close to a bullety head, a grizzling moustache on his upper lip, and a collapsible figure. His conversation was without interest or imagination; but he was evidently, as his career showed, a man of stern will and inflexible purpose. He told me that, though a German by birth, he had yet written his books on Troy and Mycenae in English, and afterwards had had them translated back into the German tongue. There was also in Athens at the time the well-known American scholar and grammarian, Professor Goodwin, of whom I find recorded in my diary the following pen portrait: "The terror of erring schoolboys, the paragon of every social virtue. In his bland exterior, handsome face, voluble delivery, and ceaseless flow of commonplace, one would not detect the acute scholar, the giant of syntax, the great formulator of the Greek $\mu\dot{\eta}$. The excessive charm of his manner could never fail to captivate; his affability nothing could disturb; but his gift of monopolising the conversation, and then turning it on to the most threadbare topics, the same stories being repeated at intervals of two days, would wear out the temper of a Moses and exhaust the patience of a Job."

We attended a debate in the Βουλή, or Chamber, on the tobacco tax. But I am ashamed to say that after listening to three-quarters of an hour of Hellenic eloquence, not even the presence in our company of a Senior Classic enabled us to identify in the modern Greek pronunciation a single word but ἀλλά – "but". Perhaps this was due to our absorption in the past, which was perpetually finding unpremeditated illustrations. For instance, when our guide told us that a great marble chair or *cathedra* which we saw in the interior of the Parthenon, belonged to the Athenian House of Lords, and had only been moved there when that institution was abolished, we felt not the faintest interest in this rather remarkable incident, until we realised that the Second Chamber in question was the old Court of the Areopagus. When the same mentor pointed to a dusty valley, which was threaded by the channel of an exhausted rivulet and told us that there were the Elysian Fields, we expressed neither satisfaction nor surprise, until we discovered that he was speaking of the

Fields that cool Ilissus laves.

And when he told us that the statue of Pallas Athene, which once stood in the Erechtheum, was so like a human being that it was said to have fallen from heaven, we thought less of its celestial origin than we did of its human sculptor.

Byron's "Maid of Athens" was reputed to have ended by marrying a policeman; and even Byron's verses experienced no better fate at our hands, as compared with the least line of the great Attic tragedians. The only point in which, at the end of our tour, we agreed that the modern Greek showed a superior intelligence to the old Greek was in his substituting for the fine masculine word ἵππος (horse), the neuter τὸ ἄλογον "the unreasoning one", an epithet which appeared to us to describe with perfect accuracy the animals that we bestrode, and of which I recorded in my diary that the only paces of which they were cognisant were "a slow and imperturbable walk, an occasional but jolting trot, a spasmodic and agonising canter, but, as for a gallop, an obstinate and incomplete incapacity."

It was, however, when we left Athens, huddled so to speak, under the umbrella of Mr. Gladstone, with Edward Lyttelton as our standard bearer, and with telegrams from Monsieur Tricoupis flying about to the nomarch of every district and the demarch of every town, bidding them extend a special welcome to the relatives of that illustrious man, equally the resuscitator of ancient and the friend of modern Greece, that our real triumphs began. Even now, at this distance of time, I can see the crowds on the quay at Nauplia and the military escort to the so-called hotel; the deputation from the aldermen and magistrates, the municipal authorities and the local Bench and Bar; Edward Lyttelton, in knickerbockers and fives shoes, rising from our humble and half-finished dinner to address the delegation in mediocre and metallic French; the receptions and dinners and entertainments at Argos and Mycenae, the cries everywhere

of Ζήτω ὁ Γλάδστων and Ζήτω τὸ Ἀγγλικὸν ἔθνος the landing at Itea on the northern shore of the Gulf of Corinth, in order to make the ascent to Delphi; the noisy reception by the massed school children at Crissa; the bonfires on the hills at night, the address from the Mayor and corporation of Kastri (the modern name of Delphi) in which our dragoman, who always translated the modern Greek into English through the medium of Italian, converted the ὦ εὐγενέστατοι ξένοι of the Mayor through the Italian equivalent of *O ingenui forestieri* into the English "O ingenuous foresters!"

The entry to Delphi was really the culminating scene. For there was produced a veteran of eighty or more years of age who had acted as a guide to Mr. Gladstone when he climbed Parnassus in the year 1856: there was also produced an aged white horse, upon which it was alleged that that renowned ascent had been made. Mounted upon this venerable steed and followed by the rest of the party on the humbler backs of mules, Lyttelton headed our procession into the ancient shrine of Apollo. First

Byron's Maid of Athens was reputed to have ended by marrying a policeman.

The ascent to Delphi was led by an aged white horse, on which Mr. Gladstone had climbed to Parnassus.

came our rather meagre cavalcade, the white horse leading with becoming gravity, and the bells on the mules tinkling bravely in the crisp air; next came the village musicians, whose instruments consisted of a melancholy pipe and a solitary drum; then the Reception Committee in loose order; next our dragoman and grinning cook, and finally two gendarmes as an evidence of the might and majesty of the Hellenic Government. As we passed along the single street of the village the old women, the matrons, and the children looked down from the many wooden balconies, waving their hands or mumbling blessings: the adult population in the street passed pomegranates and apples into our hands.

We did not, as a matter of fact, consult the oracle, which has maintained an impenetrable silence for some centuries; but even supposing that the Pythian priestess had spoken from her tripod, with her customary and unexampled command of the *double entendre*, she could not have sent us away from Delphi more contented than we were with our rustic but warm-hearted welcome.

The Voice of Memnon

As morn from Memnon drew
Rivers of melody.
TENNYSON, *The Palace of Art.*

———◆❈◆———

LONG before the *dahabeah* enters upon the great sweep of river that skirts the pylons of Karnak, the traveller has strained his eye to discover whatever traces may be visible of the once mighty city, the metropolis of an empire, and the mausoleum of its kings – Egyptian Thebes. How much or little will be remaining of the hundred temple-towers, the shrines and statues and obelisks without number, the avenues of sphinxes, the princely palaces and fortresses, the sculptured courts and colonnades? On the eastern bank the ruins of Karnak stand up in solid and monumental grandeur; but on the western the eye wanders over the level expanse that stretches to the foot of the hills, wherein lie the rifled secrets of the Tombs of the Kings, without at first encountering more than a few confused heaps or mounds, scarcely distinguishable from the sand which surrounds them. Presently, however, our gaze is arrested by two dark objects, situated at a greater distance from the river than the ruins already observed, and differing from them both in appearance and elevation. They seem to rise up like twin martellos or watch-towers from the desert, and to stand apart in melancholy solitude. The spectacle is strange and puzzling, and for a moment our imagination is at a loss for a key. Suddenly it flashes upon us that the two mysterious objects which have excited our astonishment are none other than the famed Colossi of Thebes – the Vocal Memnon and his mute companion.

A walk of a little over a mile from the river bank brings us to the base of the statues. As we approach them through the allotments of clover and maize, they loom up higher and higher, until, as we stand at their feet, their stupendous shapes almost exclude the sky. Laced on the very fringe of the cultivated soil, where the furthermost Nile deposit is cut short by the first wave of sand, they stand between the dead and the living, and seem like two grim sentinels stationed to guard the entrance to the desert behind. At other times, when the inundations are abroad and the surrounding country is turned into a sea, they tower with an even greater solemnity above the waters. The Nile stretches in an unbroken level from its own channel till it washes their pedestals and laves their massive feet. How vividly do we realise the prophet's description of "populous No, that was situate among the rivers, that had the waters round about it, whose rampart was the sea, and her wall was from the sea." It is under these conditions and at sunset that the pair should be seen. Then, as the glowing disc sinks behind the hills that enclose the Valley of the Tombs of the Kings and the dwindling radiance of the heavens is repeated in the mirror of the flood, they brood like huge black spectres over the darkening scene. Keats must have heard of this moment when he wrote:

Two dark objects rise up like twin martellos or watch-towers from the desert, and stand apart in melancholy solitude (opposite).

85

*The northernmost figure (right) is
the celebrated Vocal Memnon.*

... a vast shade
In the midst of his own brightness, like the bulk
Of Memnon's image at the set of sun
To one who travels from the dusking East.

Blacker and huger each moment the figures become, their monstrous shadows thrown forward upon the lake, till at length even the afterglow has faded, and, still as death themselves, they fitly preside over the deadly stillness of the southern night.

A closer inspection enhances rather than detracts from the majesty of the images. They are planted 54 feet apart, and face towards the south-south-east. Each represents a colossal male figure seated upon a throne, which is itself supported by a pedestal. Though the faces of both have been hacked out of all human resemblance, yet the shapeless blocks of stone seem endowed with an indefinable sentience, as if, though bereft even of the similitude of human features, their sight could pierce the endless vistas of space and time. The arms are attached to the sides and recline upon the stalwart thighs; the hands, with fingers outstretched and turned slightly inwards, are placidly disposed upon the knees; the legs, like two mighty columns, rest against the throne and lift up the lap of the

Colossus to the sky. The whole attitude is that of a giant who has sat himself down to take his repose after the fatigues and turmoil of successful war. The height of the figures is 51 feet without, and 64 feet with, the pedestal; but of the latter, 6 feet are now buried beneath the accumulations left by the Nile. Before these had been formed, and when the pedestals were bare to their foundations, when, further, each head was framed in the full spreading wig of the Egyptian Pharaohs, and when the faces and bodies were intact, the impression produced must have been such as could be felt rather than described. Between the legs of each statue are small figures of the wife and mother of the King; a figure of his daughter stands by his knee. On the two sides of the two thrones are deeply incised pictures of the Nile gods of Upper and Lower Egypt, who are plaiting together the stems of the papyrus and the lotus, the emblems of the two provinces.

Every one knows that these statues are effigies of the same King – Amunoph, or Amenhotep, or Amenophis III, one of the most famous Sovereigns and conquerors of the Eighteenth Dynasty, who reigned at Thebes about 1500 B.C., and was the husband of Queen Thiy and father of the heretic King Amenophis IV, or Akhnaton, one of whose daughters married the recently discovered Tutankhamen. The cartouches on the backs of both figures contain the King's name. Known, too, is the name of the architect – the same as that of the royal master who delighted to do him honour – Amenhotep, son of Hapu, whose own statue, richly adorned with inscriptions, is in the Boulak collection at Cairo. Thereon we read:

For my lord the King was created the monument of sandstone. Thus did I according to that which seemed best in my own eyes, causing to be made two images of a noble hard stone in his likeness in this his great building, which is like unto heaven. . . . After this manner made I perfect the King's images, wonderful for their breadth, lofty in their height, the stature whereof made the gate-tower to look small. Forty cubits was their measure. In the glorious sandstone mountain wrought I them, on this side and on that, on the east side and on the west. Furthermore, I caused to be built eight ships, whereon they were carried up and set in his lofty building. It will last as long as the heaven endureth.

From this interesting record we gather that the material of the Colossi was derived from quarries lower down the Nile, probably from those in the hills of Toora above Cairo, that they were towed or floated up the river on great barges, and were then erected before the outermost pylons of the magnificent temple which Amunoph III, in addition to his works at Luxor and Karnak, was building as a memorial of himself in the western quarter of Thebes. The famous sculpture of the Colossus on a sledge in the grotto of Ed-Dayr (so happily adapted by the late Sir E. Poynter, P.R.A., to the subject of one of his best known pictures) will give us some idea of the arduous passage of these mighty blocks, estimated as weighing 1200 tons apiece, from the river bank to their final resting-place before the pylons of the royal temple. The latter, which has perished utterly, has itself been described as "probably the greatest work of art ever wrought in Egypt."

The most superficial observation discloses several points of difference between the pair. The southernmost Colossus is a monolith, and has evidently suffered less from the hand of the destroyer than its companion, though its face and breast are mutilated beyond all recognition. The more northern statue resembles the other from the ground up to its waist, being conposed of the same dark breccia or composite stone; but its upper parts consist of five tiers of a lighter sandstone; roughly hewn, and built up one on top of the other, in rude semblance of arms and chest and head. The thrones and pedestals of both are adorned with deeply incised figures and hieroglyphics; but the feet of the northernmost are covered with a network of inscriptions in Greek and Latin, extending over the instep and reaching half-way up the leg. This latter is the celebrated Vocal Memnon.

The vocal powers so mysteriously acquired by the northern Collossus made it one of the wonders of the ancient world. Strabo says that a noise as of a slight blow was believed to issue at sunrise from the upright portion of the figure. From this time forward, a consistent series of witnesses testify to the continuance of the miracle. From the fact that the last attested instance of Memnon having spoken was in the reign of Septimius Severus, it may be inferred that something must then have happened to suspend the sound.

There they sit, the two giant brethren, scorched by the suns of more than three thousand summers, ringed by unnumbered yearly embraces of the wanton stream. By their side Stonehenge is a plaything, the work of pigmies. They are first even among the prodigies of Egypt; more solemn than the Pyramids, more sad than the Sphinx, more amazing than the pillared avenues of Karnak, more tremendous than the rock-idols of Aboo-Simbel. There they sit, patient and pathetic, their grim obliterated faces staring out into vacancy, their ponderous limbs sunk in a perpetual repose, indifferent alike to man and to Nature, careless of the sacrilege that has been perpetrated upon the mortal remains of the royal house whose glories they portrayed, steadfast while empires have crumbled and dynasties declined, serene amid all the tides of war and rapine and conquest that have ebbed and flowed from Alexandria to Assouan. There they sit and doubtless will sit till the end of all things – *sedent aeternumque sedebunt* – a wonder and a witness to men.

The Living King

When the breath of twilight blows to flame the misty skies,
All its vaporous sapphire, violet glow and silver gleam,
With their magic flood me through the gateway of the eyes:
    I am one with the twilight's dream.

                                        A. E.

MOST perfect and most graceful among the ruins of Samarkand is the cluster of mosques and mausoleums that bear the name of Shah Zindeh, the Living King. Their walls and groined ceilings are still aglow with the pageantry of the ancient tiles – ultramarine and sapphire and orange and puce, crusted over with a rich siliceous glaze, and inscribed with mighty Kufic letters. In the innermost chamber lies the coffin of the Living King, who when he lived was a near relative of the Prophet, but suffered martyrdom by decapitation in long-forgotten times. The mausoleum is ascended by steps that climb the slope of a bare and sandy hill.

Standing on the summit at the day's ending, I am a witness to one of those amazing sunsets known only in the East, when for a few seconds the earth is suffused with "the light that never was on sea or land", and then, amid a hush as of death, the twilight rushes down with violet wings and all nature swoons on her embrace. In the short space of praeternatural luminousness that precedes, the serrated edge of the Penjakent mountains cuts the sky like blue steel, and seems to sever the Zerafshan valley from the outer world. Inside the magic circle described by their lofty shapes, a splendid belt of trees plunges suddenly into a deeper and more solemn green, contrasting vividly with the purple of the mountain background.

The walls of the mosques of Shah Zindeh are aglow with ultramarine and sapphire and orange and puce.

The middle space is filled by the colossal arches and riven domes of the mosque of Bibi Khanum, "the chief wife of the Great Lord" (Timor or Tamerlane) as she was called by the Spanish Ambassador, Don Ruy de Clavijo, five centuries ago.

Gone and forgotten is she, and tottering and ruined are they, although from a distance they can be seen towering high above all the other monuments of Samarkand. Below and all around the mosque of the Living King, a waste of grey sand-hills is encumbered with the half-fallen tombstones and mouldering graves of those who have sought interment in that holy company. Here and there a horse-hair plume, floating from the end of a rickety pole, betrays the last resting-place of some nameless sheikh or saint.

In the last death-throes of the daylight, a band of turquoise blue is seen to encircle the horizon and to flush upwards towards the zenith, where light amber skeins hang entangled like the laments of a golden veil. As these drift apart and lose the transient glory, as the turquoise deepens into sapphire, and dies down into dusk; as first the belt of trees and then the outer belt of mountains is wiped out, a long cry trembles through the breathless void. It is the voice of the muezzin from the balcony of a neighbouring minaret, summoning the faithful to evening prayer.

Russia in Central Asia

IN the summer and autumn months an express train leaves Berlin at 8.30 in the morning, and reaches St. Petersburg on the evening of the following day. A traveller from England can either catch this train by taking the day boat from Queenborough to Flushing, and making the through journey without a halt, in which case he will reach the Russian capital in sixty-one hours; or by taking the night boat to Flushing, and reaching Berlin the following evening, he can allow himself the luxury of a night between the sheets before proceeding on his way. At 8.30 P.M. on the day after leaving Berlin he is deposited on the platform of the Warsaw station at St. Petersburg. The journey via St. Petersburg and Moscow is not, of course, the shortest or most expeditious route to the Caucasus and the Caspian. The quickest route, in point of time, is via Berlin to Cracow, and from there by Elisavetgrad to Kharkov on the main Russian line of railway running south from Moscow, whence the journey is continued to Vladikavkas and the Caucasus. A less fatiguing but rather longer deviation is the journey by rail from Cracow to Odessa, and thence by sea to Batoum, and train to Tiflis and Baku. A third alternative is the new overland route to Constantinople, and thence by steamer to Batoum. I travelled, however, via St. Petersburg and Moscow, partly because I wished to see those places, but mainly because I hoped at the former to obtain certain information and introductions which might be useful to me in Georgia and Transcaspia. Moreover, the stranger to Russia cannot do better than acquire his first impression of her power and importance at the seat of government, the majestic emanation of Peter's genius on the banks of the Neva.

When I left London I was assured by the representatives of the Wagon-Lits Company that all necessary arrangements had been made, that a special permit, *une autorisation spéciale*, to visit Transcaspia had been obtained, and that the rest of the party had already started from Paris. Not caring to share in the earlier movements of the excursion, which involved a delay in Europe, I proposed to join them at Vladikavkas. As soon, however, as I reached St. Petersburg I had reason to congratulate myself upon having gone to headquarters at once, for I found that matters had not been quite so smoothly arranged, and that there were formidable obstacles still to be overcome. The Russian Government is a very elaborate and strictly systematised, but also a very complicated, piece of machinery: and the motive power required to set its various parts in action is often out of all proportion to the result achieved. It would not seem to be a very serious or difficult matter to determine whether a small party – less than a dozen – of tourists should be allowed to travel over a line, the opening of which to passenger travel had been trumpeted throughout Europe, and an invitation to travel by which had originated from the director-general of the line himself. However, things are not done quite so simply at St. Petersburg. It transpired that for the permission in question the consent of five independent authorities must be sought: (1) The Governor-General of Turkestan, General Rosenbach, whose headquarters are at Tashkent; (2) the Governor-General of Transcaspia, General Komaroff, who resides at Askabad; (3) the head of the Asiatic department of the Foreign Office at St. Petersburg, M. Zinovieff; (4) the Minister of Foreign Affairs, M. de Giers, or his colleague, General Vlangali; (5) the Minister for War, General Vanoffski; the last named being the supreme and ultimate court of appeal. All these independent officials had to be consulted, and their concurrent approval obtained.

My first discovery was that not one of this number had yet signified his assent, and very grave doubts were expressed by General Vlangali, in answer to inquiries, as to the likelihood of their doing so. I even heard that the Italian Embassy had applied for leave for an officer in the Italian army, and had been point blank refused. The only Englishmen – in addition to two or three Indian officers, who, joining the railway at Tcharjui or Merv on their return from India, had travelled by it to the Caspian – to whom official permission had so far been granted were the *Times* correspondent; Dr. Lansdell, who had recently started upon another roving expedition of mingled Bible distribution and discovery in Central Asia; and Mr. Littledale, a sportsman, who had with great difficulty obtained leave to go as far as Samarkand with a view of proceeding from there in quest of the *ovis poli* in the remote mountains of the Pamir. In this pursuit I record with pleasure the fact that the last-named gentleman was entirely successful, being the first Englishman who has ever shot a male specimen of this famous and inaccessible animal. Matters were further complicated by the absence of the Minister for War, who was accompanying the Czar in his imperial progress through the south. One of my earliest steps was to seek an interview with the representative at St. Petersburg of the Compagnie des Wagon-Lits, and to inquire what steps he had taken or proposed to take. I found that he had as yet obtained no assurance of official ratification, but was relying upon the patronage and promises of General Annenkoff, who was absent and believed to be in Nice. I was, however, recommended by him to call upon M. Mestcherin, the resident engineer to the railway, who had greatly interested himself in the expedition and was doing his utmost to further its success. The first item of reassuring news that I had received fell from his lips. A telegram had been received from General Rosenbach, to whom the names of the proposed party had been submitted, signifying his approval; and another of a similar character was hourly expected from General Komaroff. This intelligence was the more satisfactory, because I heard from M. Mestcherin that it was upon General Rosenbach's supposed objections that the authorities at St. Petersburg had principally based theirs; the General's hostility being attributed to his unwillingness to have a party of foreigners anywhere near the frontier, pending the unsettled rebellion of Is-hak Khan against the Afghan Amir in a quarter of Afghan Turkestan at so short a distance from the Russian lines. I confess I regarded this as a plausible objection, though I hardly thought that the situation would be much aggravated by the casual and almost meteoric transit of a harmless party of polyglot tourists over the railway line. However, these scruples, if entertained, had now been abandoned, and the hope presented itself that the confidence displayed by General Rosenbach might awake a similar generosity in the breasts of his official superiors in the capital. M. Mestcherin had no doubt whatever that this would be the case. I left his apartments in a more sanguine frame of mind than I had yet ventured to indulge. Nevertheless, the fact that there had lately been an accident on the line, owing apparently to its imperfect construction, in which more persons than one were said to have been killed, and the rumoured total breakdown of the bridge over the Oxus at Tcharjui, were discouraging omens, and suggested a possible explanation for the reluctance of the Russian official world to admit the inquisitive eyes of strangers. These were arguments, however, which could have no weight with General Annenkoff, who was credited with an absolute confidence in the capacities of his staff, and whose cosmopolitan sympathies I had no reason to question.

General Annenkoff whose cosmopolitan sympathies I had no reason to question.

The doubts which had arisen as to the prospects of my journey were still unsolved when I left St. Petersburg; while at Moscow they were yet further aggravated by the information which I received from headquarters. I was advised on the highest authority not to persevere in the attempt, and was warned that in any case an answer could not be expected for a considerable time. Subsequently to this I even heard that our names had been submitted to the War Minister, who had declined to sanction them, which refusal was further declared to be irrevocable. In spite of this ominous dissuasion, which I had some ground for believing to be due to a jealousy between the departments of the Foreign Office and War Office at St. Petersburg, I decided to start from Moscow, and did so after waiting there for six days. It was not till I reached Vladikavkas, on the Caucasus, three days later, that a telegraphic despatch conveyed to me the unexpected and welcome tidings that permission had after all been conceded, and that the entire party, the rest of whom were now assembled in a state of expectancy at Tiflis, might proceed across the Caspian. All is well that ends well; and I am not any longer concerned to explore the tortuous windings of diplomatic policy or official intrigue at St. Petersburg. General Annenkoff had assured us that we should be allowed to go, and leave having been given, with him undoubtedly remained the honours of war. Later on we heard that the Minister for War, upon seeing the permission of Generals Rosenbach and Komaroff, had at once given his consent without even informing the Foreign Office. Conceive the feelings of the latter!

Were I writing a narrative of travel, I might invite my readers to halt with me for a few moments at St. Petersburg, at Moscow, at Nijni-Novgorod, in the Caucasus, at Tiflis, or at Baku. I stayed in each of these places, exchanging the grandiose splendour and civilised smartness of

The Oriental irregularity and bizarre beauty of Moscow.

the capital – with its architecture borrowed from Italy, its amusements from Paris, and its pretentiousness from Berlin – for the Oriental irregularity and bizarre beauty of Moscow, an Eastern exotic transplanted to the West, an inland Constantinople, a Christian Cairo. No more effective illustration could be furnished of the Janus-like character of this huge political structure, with its vast unfilled courts and corridors in the east, and, as Peter the Great phrased it, its northern window looking out upon Europe, than the outward appearance of its two principal cities, the one a Western plagiarism, the other an Asiatic original. Through the Caucasus we drove, four horses abreast attached to a kind of family barouche, by the famous Dariel Road. Piercing one of the finest gorges in Europe, it climbs a height of 8,000 ft., and skirts the base of a height of 16,000 ft. This is the celebrated pass that drew a line to the conquests alike of Alexander and Justinian, the Caucasian Gates of the ancient world, which shut off the East on this side from the West, and were never owned at entrance and exit by the same Power till they fell into Russia's hands. Above them tower the mighty rocks of Kazbek on which the tortured Prometheus hung, and away to the right is Elbruz, the *doyen* of European summits. This road is for the present at any rate, and will probably long remain, of the highest military importance, as it is the first line of communication both with Armenia and the Caspian; and its secure tenure dispenses with the delays of transport and navigation by the Black Sea. Though skilfully engineered, substantially metalled, and constantly repaired (relays of soldiers being employed in the winter to cut a passage through the snows), it cannot be compared for evenness or solidity with the roads which the British have made in similar surroundings in many parts of the world. It debouches 135 miles from Vladikavkas upon Tiflis, where the traveller begins to realise that though still in the same country he has changed continents. There I found the rest of the party assembled, consisting of two Englishmen, three Frenchmen, an Italian, and a Dutchman. With an Englishman, a Pole, and a Mingrelian, to whom was subsequently added a Tajik of Bokhara, as our guides and conductors, we constituted about as representative a body as General Annenkoff in his most cosmopolitan of moments would have desired.

At Tiflis we received from General Sheremétieff, acting governor in the absence of Prince Dondoukoff Korsakoff, who had gone to meet the Emperor, the official document, or *oktriti list*, authorising us to cross the Caspian and to travel in the Russian dominions in Central Asia. The ordinary passport through viséed and counter-viséed is useless east of the Caspian, and many a traveller, straining its limited sanctity, has been turned back from the regions to which the *oktriti list* alone will procure admission. With this magical piece of paper in our possession we started without any further delay by the single daily train, that leaving Tiflis at ten in the evening arrives at Baku between four and five on the following afternoon. There we spent a day inspecting the peculiar features of the place and visiting the works of Balakhani, some eight miles from the town, where a forest of tall wooden towers like chimney-stacks marks the site of the deep wells from which the crude naphtha either springs in spontaneous jets from hidden subterranean sources, or is drawn up by steam power in long cylindrical tubes, and despatched to the distilleries in the town. Of this petroleum industry which has reached the most gigantic proportions, I will say nothing here; I have the incentive to silence that, of previous visitors who have described their journey to Transcaspia, scarcely one has resisted the temptation to speech. At 5.30 in the afternoon we put off from the wharf in the steamboat "Prince Bariatinski", belonging to the Caucasus and Mercury Company, which was frequently impressed by Skobeleff and his troops in the Turkoman campaigns of 1879, 1880, and 1881. As we steamed out on the placid waters of the Caspian, whose surface far out to sea gleamed daily under the metallic lustre of the floating oil, the setting sun lit up an altar of fire behind the pink cliffs of the Apsheron peninsula, which would have turned to ridicule the most prodigal devotion, even in their palmiest days, of the defunct fire-worshippers of Baku. On the other side a leaden canopy of smoke overhung the petroleum works, and the dingy quarters of the manufacturing town.

At sunrise on the next morning rocky land was visible to the north-east. This was the mountainous background to Krasnovodsk, the first Russian settlement twenty years ago on the eastern shore of the Caspian,

The works of Balakhani some eight miles from the town, where the petroleum industry has reached gigantic proportions.

and the original capital of the province of Transcaspia. Thither the terminus of the railway is likely to be transferred from Uzun Ada, on account of the shallow and shifting anchorage at the latter place. Later on low sandhills, clean, yellow, and ubiquitous, fringed the shore or were distributed in melancholy islets over the surface of the bay. The whole appearance of the coast is strikingly reminiscent of a river delta, a theory which is in close harmony with the admitted geological fact that the Oxus once emptied itself by one at least of its mouths or tributaries into the Balkan Bay. Soon we entered a narrow channel, at the extremity of which the masts of ships, the smoking funnels of steamers, and several projecting wooden piers and wharves indicated a position of considerable commercial activity; and at 2.30 p.m. were moored to the landing stage of Uzun Ada, on which appeared to be gathered the entire population of the settlement, whose sole distraction the arrival and departure of the steamer must be. This is the present starting point of the Transcaspian Railway.

From the Caspian to Merv

To Margiana from the Hyrcanian cliffs
Of Caucasus, and dark Iberian dales.
MILTON, *Paradise Regained*, 317.

UZUN Ada, where we landed on the eastern shore of the Caspian and which was made the western terminus of the railway in August 1886, is certainly not an attractive or inspiring spot, though it perhaps hardly deserves the savage abuse with which it has been assailed, any more than it does the laudatory exaggeration of French and Russian scribes. The word means Long Island, and the town is accordingly built on a low and straggling islet of sand, the yellow of which glitters fiercely between the opposite blues of sky and sea. There is not a blade of grass or a drop of water to be seen, and the heat in the summer months must be appalling. The town consists of a number of small wooden houses and shops (children must be born and exist at Uzun Ada, because I actually saw a toy shop) reared in a promiscuous fashion on the sand, which is elsewhere covered with sheds, warehouses, and other large wooden buildings.

Most of the houses arrived, ready made, in numbered blocks, from Astrakhan, where they had cost 60*l*. apiece. A freight charge of 12*l*., and

Uzun Ada is certainly not an attractive or inspiring spot.

97

Fixing the telegraph wires near Uzun Ada.

The famous Kara Kum or Black Sand. So hard is the surface in dry weather that a camel will barely leave the impression of its footmark.

a further 3*l*. for the expenses of erection, raised the actual figure to 75*l*. each. The more important buildings were constructed upon the spot with material brought from Russia. I could see the reservoir and engine-house where the condensation of seawater is effected; and though the bulk of the water supply arrives by train every day from the interior, I observed signs that these artificial agencies were still in use. The piers were loaded with bales of cotton and other merchandise, and a good deal of business appeared to be going on. Uzun Ada is, however, though preferable to Michaelovsk, a very unsatisfactory anchorage; for it contains only from 10 to 12 feet of water, and is constantly silting up, the channel requiring to be kept open by dredges; whilst in winter the bay is sometimes thickly frozen over and quite inaccessible to navigation. It is not surprising therefore to hear that a commission has sat and reported in favour of moving the landing-place to the old harbour of Krasnovodsk, 80 miles to the north, where the greater distance is compensated by an ample depth of water and by excellent facilities for disembarkation. As soon as the line begins to pay its way, we may expect to see the removal effected. The flimsy and ephemeral character of the present town, which only numbers about 800 inhabitants, will then be seen to have harmonised both with its sudden and mechanical origin and with its abrupt demise; and Uzun Ada will vanish from existence, unwept and unhonoured, if not altogether unsung.

The railway station is at the distance of a few hundred yards from the landing-stage; and the traveller ploughs his way to the platform (which

The train crosses a long embankment of 1,300 yards, by which the islet is united to the mainland (top left).

Uzun Ada will vanish from existence, unwept and unhonoured, if not altogether unsung (top right)

As soon as the line begins to pay its way, we may expect to see the removal of the town effected (bottom).

does not exist) through an ankle-depth of sand. Four hours are allowed for an exhaustive inspection of the local features, or are more probably intended as a tribute to the possible delays of the Caspian. Finally the train starts, crosses a long embankment of 1,300 yards, by which the islet is united to the mainland, and plunges into the sullen dunes of the desert.

A funereal tale of destruction, both to man and beast, engulfed in their whirling crests, might these cruel sand-waves tell; and the bones of many a victim lie trampled fathoms deep under the pitiless tide. The peaks of the great Balkan range on the north, rising in points to a height of 5,000 ft., afford a welcome relief to the eye, and, after a wide depression in the surface level, through which the Oxus or one of its confluents once disembogued into the Caspian, are succeeded by the inferior elevation of the Little Balkans on the south. These are presently merged in the splendid barrier of the Persian mountains, which, first under the name of the Kuren Dagh, with an average height of 1,500 to 2,000 ft., and later on, while the elevation increases, as the Kopet Dagh, rising to 5,000 and 6,000 ft. and even higher, overhang the railway, with an axis inclined from north-west to south-east, for nearly 300 miles, till their southern spurs are confounded in the mountains of Gulistan. On their far side, just over the summit, runs the Persian frontier, which was fixed by the treaty with Russia in December 1881, and has been demarcated by commissioners since. Very grand and impressive these mountains are, with an outline ever original and new, and with grey flanks scoured by deep oval gullies, either torn by the irresistible action of water or representing the depressions between the immemorial geological folds of the mountains as they emerged from the superincumbent sea. One is the more inclined to the former view from the recent experience of the railway itself, which has twice during the last three months been bodily swept away for some distance by one of these terrific rushes, descending from the hills after a sudden storm.

If the mountains on the south supply a perpetual variety of shape and summit, there is a more than equivalent monotony in the spectacle that extends as far as the eye can reach to the north. Here nothing is visible but a wide and doleful plain, wholly destitute, or all but destitute, of vegetation, and sweeping with unbroken uniformity to a blurred horizon. This desert is the famous Kara Kum or Black Sand, which, with intervals of dunes and interruptions of so-called oases, stretches from the Caspian to the Oxus, and from Khorasan to Khiva and the Aral Sea. Originally part of the old Aralo-Caspian basin, it has, partly by an upheaval of surface, partly by the action of air-currents, been converted into an utter wilderness. In its worst parts, and they are at first the more frequent, it consists of a perfectly level expanse, plastered over with marl, which is cracked and blistered by the sun, and is covered with a thin top-dressing of saline crystallisation. So hard is the surface in dry weather that a camel will barely leave the impression of its footmark, and the torrents from the mountains, unable to penetrate the crust, lie outspread in lakes and pools. That this sorrowful waste was once at the bottom of the sea is proved by the numerous specimens of Aralo-Caspian mollusc fauna that

Uzun Ada built on a low and struggling islet of sand (centre). The sand dunes through which the train plunges into the sullen dunes of the desert (middle back). Kopet Dagh, a splendid barrier rising to 5,000 to 6,000 ft (bottom). Kara Kum across which the water supply travels by train.

102

have been found imbedded in the sand; but I do not suppose that their value would induce even the most austere pupil of science to veto a proposal, were such within the bounds of possibility, for the resumption of the *status quo ante* on its part. The desiccated gulfs and channels which in some portions furrow its surface, after supplying an innocent pastime to a generation of theorists, are now generally understood to mark, not former beds of the Oxus, but the ancient shore-line of a much larger Caspian.

At intervals this desert is broken by belts of more or less cultivable soil, which, under the modest standards of so barren a country, are dignified by the name of oases. There are four such oases between Uzun Ada and the Oxus, viz. those of Akhal, Atek (or the mountain base), Tejend, and Merv. An oasis in these parts has no relation to the *a priori* picture, painted by our imagination, in which rivulets of water course through a wealth of verdure beneath umbrageous trees. It is simply a designation for such portions of the desert as have been reclaimed, by moisture naturally or artificaly supplied, for the service of man; the extent of their fertility depending entirely upon the poverty or abundance of the streams. Geologically their surface consists of a layer of alluvial soil, which has been washed down by rain and snow from the easily disintegrated face of the mountains, and has formed a deposit along the base. In places the fertility has been increased by the natural action of the later geological periods.

There is a good deal of variety in the vegetation of these oases. In the more sterile parts they seem to support little but a stunted growth of tamarisk, absinthe, camelthorn, and light desert shrubs; though even here in the spring-time there is a sudden and magical efflorescence of bright prairie flowers. With the torrid summer heats these swiftly fade and die, and the abomination of desolation then sets in. Elsewhere, under the influence of a richer water supply, barley, rice, maize, millet, sorghum, and lucerne are succeeded in the most fertile districts by orchards and gardens, which produce an amazing crop of melons, apricots, peaches and grapes.

Kizil Arvat, the original terminus of the railway, which is the first important place we reach, and which has 2,000 inhabitants, and, what is even more remarkable, a fountain playing at the station, is commonly described as marking the beginning of the Akhal oasis, the belt of country inhabited by that tough race of brigands, whose long career of raid and pillage was summarily extinguished at Geok Tepe by Skobeleff in 1881. Of this oasis, which extends for a length of between 150 and 200 miles with varying fertility, the Turkomans have a proverb that says: "Adam when driven forth from Eden never found a finer place for settlement than Akhal"; a boast, the vanity of which is not untempered with discretion, seeing that it stops short of the assertion that he ever *did* settle there. For this unexpected modesty the traveller in a strange country may well feel grateful.

Through an entire day we traversed this plain, the features of which become positively fatiguing in their shameless uniformity. Clustered

here and there are to be seen the kibitkas or circular tents of the Turkomans, who have been tempted back to their old hunting-grounds. But these, which represent the peaceful life of the present, cannot be compared in number with the small clay watch-towers, dotted about like pepper-pots all over the expanse, and the rectangular walled forts and enclosures with towers at the corners, which recall the fierce unsettled existence, the dreaded *alamans* or raids, and the turbulent manners of the past. Occasionally are to be seen great circular tumuli here called *Kurgans*, which are supposed either to be the milestones of forgotten nomad advance or the cemeteries of the still more forgotten dead. Some are circular and others oval in shape; they are sometimes 40 or 50 feet high, with steep sides, and a circumference at the base of 200 or 300 yards. Ever and anon a solitary sand-column, raised by a passing puff of air, starts up, and giddily revolving on its fragile axis whirls away over the plain. This spectacle extends to the northern horizon, where it is lost in the mirage which is prevalent in these parts, and the liquid tremulous medium of which transforms the featureless dismal plain into luscious lakes of water with floating islets of trees. Often were the soldiers of

*The Persian mountains overhang the railway for nearly 300 miles (top).
More trains of water cisterns bound for Uzun Ada (bottom).*

105

Skobeleff's brigades deceived and disappointed by this never-stale conjuring trick of the desert; and the oldest traveller would probably confess to having succumbed to its ever-green illusion.

Among the remarkable features of this tract of country, none is more extraordinary than the variations of climate, which in their violent extremes are out of all proportion to the latitude in which it lies, the same as that of Smyrna, of Lisbon, and of San Francisco. In summer the heat is that of a seven times heated furnace, and the scanty water-sources are insufficient to sustain life. The winter cold is sometimes Arctic; entire herds of cattle are frozen to death in the steppes; a deep snow covers the ground to the depth of two or three feet; and many human lives are lost in the storms. The past winter (1888-9), for instance, has been one of uncommon severity: the thermometer registered 20 degrees (Réaumur) of frost; water was sold along the railway at 2s, a pailful; and the needs of fuel have wrought shocking havoc among the rapidly dwindling supplies of the Saxaoul. These climatic vicissitudes render campaigning in any but the spring and autumn months of the year a very precarious venture, and might abruptly suspend the most successful military operations. The campaign of Geok Tepe could not have reached so speedy and favourable an issue but for the abnormal mildness of the winter of 1880-1, when the stars in their courses fought for Skobeleff.

We passed Bahmi, a place once of some little importance, and at 2.30 on the afternoon of the day after leaving the Caspian stopped at the station of Geok Tepe, about sixty yards from the mouldering ruins of the famous Tekke fortress. Looking out of the window beforehand, we had already caught sight of the western face of the great rampart, and of a small fort outside where were trees and some mills worked by the Tekkes during the siege with the aid of the stream that entered the encampment from this quarter. Towering above the outer wall we could also see in the north-western corner a lofty mound, which was used as a post of observation and as a battery by the besieged. The entire enclosure, which is still fairly perfect, measured 2 miles 1,275 yards in circuit, and the walls of rammed clay – though crumbling to ruin and though stripped of their upper half immediately after the capture in order to cover the bodies of the thousands of slain – are still on the average about twelve feet high. In their face are to be seen the holes scooped out by the shells which imbedded themselves uselessly in the earthy mass; and on the side running parallel with the line are still the two breaches on either side of the S.E. angle which were created by the Russian mines. In the centre is the main exit, masked by an outer fortification, from which the impetuous sallies were made that four times swept down like a tornado upon the Russian camp. The latter was to the south of the site now occupied by the station, and between it and the mountains, from the top of one of which, on January 24, 1881, Edmund O'Donovan, striving to push his way to Skobeleff's army, and reaching the crest at the critical moment, looked down as from a balloon upon a distant assault, and watched through his field-glass the crowd of fugitives as they streamed in the agony of flight across the plain. I have always thought this one of the most dramatic

incidents of modern history. Clambering up the ruined bank, I found that it consisted of a double wall the whole way round, or rather of a single wall of enormous breadth, between the lofty battlements of which on the top was a place where men were placed to fire at the besiegers, and where, when the fortress was stormed, many of them were found sitting as they had been shot perhaps days before, with their bodies pierced by bullets, and their heads fallen forward between their knees. The bones of camels, and sometimes of men, may still be seen lying within the desolate enclosure; and for long after the assault and capture, it was impossible to ride over the plain without the horse-hoofs crushing into human skulls. Visiting this interesting spot in the company of an eye-witness of the siege, who was brought into frequent personal contact with the Commander-in-Chief, I was made acquainted with details about the storming of the fortress, as well as about the personality of the extraordinary man who conducted it, that have not found their way into the works dealing with either subject.

The main incidents of the siege and capture of Geok Tepe are well known, and may be read in the official report of General Skobeleff, which was translated into English, and published in this country in 1881. In March, 1880, Skobeleff was appointed to the chief command. Having made a preliminary reconnaissance of the Turkoman position in July of the same year, he retired to the Caspian, completed his preparations there, and in December returned with about 7,000 men and over 60 guns to invest the fortress, the correct name of which was Denghil Tepe, Geok Tepe being the title of a small settlement a little further in the desert. Having first cleared the Turkomans out of the fortified redoubt of Yenghi Kala at the foot of the cliffs, he pitched his own camp there at a distance of a mile from the main position at Denghil Tepe, within which were gathered, under the command of Makdum Kuli Khan and his general, Tekme Sirdar, since dead, the flower of the Akhal Tekkes, with their wives and families – some 35,000 persons, assisted by 10,000 horsemen. Between the 1st and the 24th of January, a first, a second, and finally a third parallel of siege works were laid; enfilading batteries were erected to rake the interior of the fort; four desperate sallies of the besieged, made under cover of darkness, were successfully repelled; and the Russian lines were steadily pushed forward till at last they were so close that the Russian officers walking to and from the council tent were fired at, that lights were forbidden at night because they attracted a hail of bullets, and that wounded men in the ambulance tents were shot again as they lay. Some of the troops were in the trenches, where also Skobeleff's tent was pitched; he courted every risk himself, and was never so gratified as when he heard that his officers had been in serious danger and under fire. When the Russians began to dig their mines for the final assault, their advanced redoubt was only 70 yards from the Tekke ramparts, and the troops in the foremost trenches could actually hear the Turkomans talking together on the walls, and wondering what their opponents were doing, poking their snouts like pigs into the ground. Russian sentinels on the watch-towers frequently overheard the discussions and ejaculations of the besieged, and reported to the general the waning spirit of the defence. Nevertheless the Tekkes fought with amazing desperation and courage. They would creep out from the fort at night, crawl over the sand, lying motionless perhaps for hours in the same position, and finally steal the Russian rifles, piled right under the noses of the sentinels, and glide stealthily away.

On the 20th of January, breaching operations commenced, and part of the wall was knocked down by artillery, but was as quickly repaired by the besieged. Finally the two mines, easterly and westerly, were ready; the former was charged with over a ton of gunpowder; and at 1 A.M. on the morning of the 24th, Lieutenant Ostolopoff and Naval Cadet Meyer volunteered to carry a charge of gun-cotton to the walls and explode it in the western breach which had already been battered open by the cannon fire. This feat was successfully performed. Meyer was shot by a bullet through the face, but ultimately recovered, and with the aid of an artificial palate can still speak.

On the morning of the 24th the troops were in position at 6 A.M. The attacking force was divided into three columns, under Colonels Kuropatkin, Kozelkoff, and Haidaroff, advancing two from the south, and one from the west. At 7 A.M. the breaching battery reopened fire with thirty-six guns upon the old breach and soon knocked it down again, the shells crashing through the aperture into the densely packed interior, where they wrought fearful destruction. At 11.20 the gunpowder mine was sprung on the S.E. face; a prodigious column of mingled dust and smoke shot high into the air, and, falling, disclosed a yawning cavity fifty yards wide. At the same instant the soldiers of the two main storming columns, shouting "hurrah", rushed at the gap, where a terrific hand-to-hand fight was waged with bayonet, lance, and sword. Reserves came up from the rear, with bands playing, drums beating, and colours flying, to support the attack.

Simultaneously, the third column, with the aid of scaling ladders, stormed the western face of the fort. Inside was to be seen a sea of tents and a panic-stricken but desperate crowd. From the opposite direction thousands of fugitives streamed out on to the plain; but all through the day more resolute spirits, concealed in huts or holes inside the enclosure, continued to start out and fire at the victorious enemy. Boulangier, in his book, speaking of the assault, says, "At this solemn moment Skobeleff shone so splendidly in the eyes of his men, that he seemed to their imagination to be a type of the god of war." As a matter of fact it was rather difficult either for Skobeleff to shine on this occasion, or for his men to see him; for he took no part in the attack himself, but, as a prudent general should, directed the operations from the rear. Boulangier's phrase was based on a misunderstanding of an account which Dr. Heyfelder had given him of a mimic repetition of the assault which Skobeleff ordered a few weeks later for the entertainment of a distinguished Persian khan, and which he led with boyish enthusiasm himself. Within less than an hour of the assault, the three columns had joined ranks inside the fort; and in close formation, with massed bands, advanced to the hill of Denghil Tepe, from which at 1 P.M. the two-headed eagle, fluttering in the breeze, proclaimed a Russian victory.

Then ensued the least credible episode of the entire campaign. At four in the afternoon Skobeleff led his cavalry through the breach and ordered both horse and foot to pursue the retreating enemy and to give no quarter. This command was obeyed with savage precision by both till darkness fell – by the infantry (six companies) for a distance of seven miles, by the cavalry (a division of dragoons and four *sotnias* of Cossacks) for eleven miles, supported by a battery of horse artillery with long range guns. Eight thousand persons of both sexes and all ages were mercilessly cut down and slain. "On the morning after the battle they lay in rows like freshly mown hay, as they had been swept down by the mitrailleuses and cannon." In the fort were found the corpses of 6,500 men, and some thousands of living women and children. There too, in General Grodekoff's own words, "all who had not succeeded in escaping were killed to a man by the Russian soldiers, the only males spared being the Persian prisoners, who were easily recognised by the fetters on their legs, and of whom there were about 600 in all. After that only women and children, to the number of about 5,000, were left." The troops were allowed to loot without interruption for four days, and booty to the value of 600,000l. was found inside the fortress. In the operations of the day the Russian loss was only 60 killed and 340 wounded; during the entire campaign 283 killed and 689 wounded. Within the same time Skobeleff admitted that he must have destroyed 20,000 of the enemy.

It was not a rout, but a massacre; not a defeat, but extirpation; and it is not surprising that after this drastic lesson, the Tekkes of the Akhal oasis have never lifted a little finger against their conquerors.

An incident related to me in Transcaspia afforded an interesting corroboration of the immeasurable effect that was produced upon the inhabitants by this disastrous day. I have already narrated that the Russian columns advanced to the assault with drums beating and bands playing, a favourite plan of Skobeleff's whenever he attacked. Five years later, when the railway was opened to Askabad, and in the course of the inaugural ceremonies the Russian military music began to play, the Turkoman women and children raised woeful cries of lamentation, and the men threw themselves on the ground with their foreheads in the dust.

For the horrible carnage that followed upon the capture of Geok Tepe, Skobeleff and the Russians cannot escape reproach. The former, though generous and merciful towards his own men, had no pity for an enemy. To an utter contempt for human life he joined a physical excitement on the battlefield, by which his followers as well as himself were transported. It was written of him that "he rode to battle clad in white, decked with orders, scented and curled, like a bridegroom to a wedding, his eyes gleaming with wild delight, his voice tremulous with joyous excitement." War was to him the highest expression of human force; and in action he seemed to acquire a perfect lust for blood. The Turkomans called him *Guenz Kanli*, or Bloody Eyes, and his presence inspired them with a superstitious terror. When organising his forces before the campaign he particularly requested that no officers with humanitarian ideas should be sent to the front. In a letter to the chief of the staff of the Caucasus Military District he wrote as follows:

The hard necessities of war are everywhere alike, and the steps taken by Lomakin (in September 1879) require no justification. There is no doubt as to this in my own mind, or as to the soldier being permitted to have no opinions of his own in such matters, and being solely obliged to obey orders. I must ask you, for the good of the service, and for the sake of the duty entrusted to me, only to send me officers whose sole idea is their duty, and who do not entertain visionary sentiments.

After Geok Tepe had fallen and the rout was over, he remarked: "How unutterably bored I am, there is nothing left to do." His own cruelty was not shared by many of his men, who, when the fight was over, might be seen walking about, holding the little fatherless Tekke children by the hand. I have narrated or revived these incidents, because, repellent though they be to nineteenth-century notions, and discreditable to the Russian character, they do not stand alone in the history of Russian Conquest in Central Asia, but are profoundly characteristic of the methods of warfare by which that race has consistently and successfully set about the subjugation of Oriental peoples.

Skobeleff himself candidly expressed it as follows: "I had it as a principle that in Asia the duration of peace is in direct proportion to the slaughter you inflict upon the enemy. The harder you hit them the longer they will be quiet afterwards. My system is this: To strike hard, and keep on hitting till resistance is completely over; then at once to form ranks, cease slaughter, and be kind and humane to the prostrate enemy." A greater contrast than this can scarcely be imagined to the British method, which is to strike gingerly a series of taps, rather than a downright blow; rigidly to prohibit all pillage or slaughter, and to abstain not less wholly from subsequent fraternisation. But there can be no doubt that the Russian tactics, however deficient they may be from the moral, are exceedingly effective from the practical point of view; and that an Oriental people in particular, on whose memory has been stamped the print of some such terrible disaster, are disposed to recognise in the heavy hand of the conqueror the all-powerful will of God, and to pass at once from furious antagonism to peaceful and even friendly submission.

Of Skobeleff's character and nature many stories are still told by those who were brought into contact with him in this campaign. He was one of those rare spirits who, like Napoleon, exercised a magnetic influence over other men, and the mere sight of whose white uniform, flashing like the plume of Henry of Navarre, electrified his troops on the field of combat. A hundred exploits testify to his magnificent courage and insensibility to danger. He had only twice been wounded in his life, and frequently declared, "The bullet does not exist that can strike me down." On one occasion, before Geok Tepe, he was leisurely surveying the fortress amid a storm of bullets, when the staff-surgeon joined him. "This is no place for you," said Skobeleff, "I order you to go." The surgeon protested that by the general's side he considered himself safe. "I am invulnerable," was the reply, "but if you do not go, well, I will immediately put you under arrest." The surgeon having retired, Skobeleff then took a seat, and calmly sat down to continue his observations amid the fire of the enemy.

In the Turkoman campaign he declined to allow any newspaper correspondents with his force – a decision but for which poor O'Donovan would probably never have had either the temptation or the opportunity to strike out for Merv – and did not have a single newspaper sent after him to the front. As a commander, though severe upon others, he set a most dangerous example himself, for he knew no discipline, and just as he had disobeyed the commands of his superior officers in the Turkish war, so he neglected the orders of the Emperor in the Turkoman campaign. Nevertheless, a general at thirty, and a popular idol when he succumbed to a discreditable end at the early age of thirty-eight, it is impossible to say if he had lived what he might not have done or have become.

His private character was more eccentric still – a curious jumble of nobility and meanness, of manly attributes, and of childish temper. At one time he was bold, imperious, inspired; at another, querulous and morose; now sanguine, now despondent, changing his mood, like a chameleon its colour, half a dozen times in the day. Even his friends were made the victims of these Protean transformations, being alternately treated with affection and contempt. The transition would be reflected in his countenance, which was now beautiful, now ugly, and in his physical condition, which oscillated between masculine vigour and nervous exhaustion. After Geok Tepe he was ill for some weeks, and, though always on horseback, yet after a long ride he would return so prostrated that he almost fell from his saddle, and had to retire to his bed for days. He was a magnificent figure mounted, and was proud of his horses, which were always white or grey, as he had a passion for that colour, and even forgave a personal enemy who with true diplomacy presented him with a fine white charger bought for the purpose in Moscow. But his horses were not safer from his incurable caprice than were his friends. For when on one occasion after the fall of Geok Tepe the grey Persian which he was riding into the fort refused to cross the little canal that flowed into the camp, he gave it away at once, and never mounted it again. His unscrupulousness is well illustrated by the episode with which he commenced his public career. Then a young officer of hussars in Turkestan, and burning for distinction, he presented a report to Kaufmann, the Governor-General, upon the successful suppression of a horde of brigands on the Bokharan frontier, in which he claimed to have killed over forty of the bandits. The whole thing subsequently turned out to be a myth, there being no brigands at all.

Two anecdotes I heard in Transcaspia which afford not a bad illustration of his wayward and ill-balanced nature. After the fall of Geok Tepe, a Russian general arrived from the Grand Duke Michael, at that time Governor-General of the Caucasus, to inspect the camp and troops, and to make a report. This officer, General Pavloff by name, had originally been appointed, after the death of General Petrusevitch, to replace Skobeleff, if the latter were killed; but arriving at Krasnovodsk on the very day of the fall of Geok Tepe, he was instructed to proceed in order to discuss with the Commander-in-Chief the future settlement of the oasis. Skobeleff was very angry indeed, because this officer, though of inferior military rank to himself (he having been promoted for the affair of Geok Tepe), would yet take precedence of him on this occasion as the representative of the Grand Duke. Accordingly he did his best to shirk a meeting altogether, and was infuriated when, the general having fallen ill at Bahmi, he was at length compelled to go and meet him, and above all to go in a carriage, a thing which he had never before done in time of war. The general proposed that they should both retire in Krasnovodsk to discuss the question of decorations, &c. Then the patience of Skobeleff broke down, or rather his unscrupulous resourcefulness came in. A telegram suddenly arrived with the news that 6,000 Tekkes were advancing from Merv. It was, of course, impossible for him to proceed to Krasnovodsk; he must return at once to the camp. Orders were given for an expedition to be prepared; the medical staff was required to get ready; and some regiments which were to leave for Russia on the next day, and had made all their preparations for departure, were countermanded at the last moment. Meanwhile the luckless general, who was the *fons et origo mali*, had retired alone to the Caspian. When he was well off the scene of action Skobeleff's cheerfulness revived. "Let us wait a little," he said; "possibly the telegram may not be true." And sure enough another telegram soon followed saying that it was not 6,000 but 600 Tekkes who were on the way, and that they were coming, not to attack the Russian camp, but to seek their families and friends. The curious thing was, not that the trick succeeded, but that every soldier in the force knew that it had been played by Skobeleff, and admired him none the less.

A few weeks after the storming of Geok Tepe, a distinguished Persian Khan, the Governor or Ilkhani of Kuchan, whose full name was Shuja ud Daulat Amir Hussein Khan, rode into the camp with an escort of 300 Persians to congratulate Skobeleff on his victory. The latter, who was in a pet, and did not want to be bored with entertainment, his thoughts being centred in an advance upon Merv, had already ridden off to Lutfabad, leaving his guest to the care of his staff. The eminent Persian was very much offended at this want of respect, and speaking at a banquet said that he had come to compliment the Russian commander, but as the commander was not forthcoming he must depart. An aide-de-camp at once galloped off with this ultimatum to Skobeleff, who presently turned up much against his will, and organised for the Khan the mimic assault to which I have before alluded. In the evening a dinner was given in his honour. The meal, however, had hardly commenced when an officer arrived from St. Petersburg, bringing a decoration for Skobeleff and despatches from the Emperor. Hastily deserting his place by the Khan, with the feigned excuse of feeling a draught, Skobeleff commissioned an officer of inferior rank to fill his seat, while he himself moved to a place lower down to chat with the new arrival from St. Petersburg. Presently the Khan, being very much insulted, rose and said "Goodnight". Skobeleff then made excuses for his breach of manners, but, remembering the draught, found himself unable to return to the head of the table. The story, which I heard from an eye witness, is interesting only as an illustration of his whimsical and petulant temper.

If we were to sum up his character – and I have laid stress upon it, as that of the only really commanding personality whom the history of Russian advance in Central Asia has produced – we might conclude that, though a greatly gifted, Skobeleff was not a great man, being deficient in stability, in principle, and in faith. In many respects his character was typical of the Russian nation, in its present phase of development, with one foot, so to speak, planted in a barbarian past, while the other is advancing into a new world of ideas and action. To many it will seem that he died in a happy hour, both for his country, which might have suffered from his insensate levity and passion for war, and for himself, seeing that his reputation, which a premature death has now enshrined in legend, might not have permanently survived the touchstone of truth. Russian writers are very sensitive indeed of criticism upon one who was both a political idol and the darling of the army. But foreigners are, perhaps, better able than his own countrymen to ascertain the true perspective of this meteoric phenomenon. They may confess, what the ardour of a patriot might tempt him to conceal, that the light which it shed, though often dazzling, was sometimes lurid.

Between Geok Tepe and the capital, Askabad, a distance of about twenty-eight miles, the railway passes through a country of more extensive cultivation and greater fertility. Tending their flocks, or riding on horses or asses, are to be seen numerous Turkomans, father and son sometimes bestriding the same animal. In these peaceful and unimposing rustics, who would divine the erewhile scourge and man-hunter of the desert? Clad in his dilapidated cotton dressing-gown or *khalat*, and with a huge brown sheepskin bonnet, almost as big as a grenadier's bearskin, overshadowing his dusky features, he does not perhaps look like a civilised being, but still less would you take him for a converted Dick Turpin or Claude Duval. Excellent agriculturists these ancient moss-troopers are said to be, and now that the heyday of licence and war and plunder has faded into a dream, they settle down to a peasant's existence with as much contentment as they formerly leaped to saddle for a foray on the frontiers of Khorasan.

Askabad, which we next reach, has all the appearance of a large and flourishing place. Its station is of European proportions and appointment. Numbers of droshkies attend the arrival of the trains; and the crowded platform indicates a considerable population. I was informed that the present figures are 10,000; but these, which I believe to be an exaggerated estimate, include the troops, of which there are three rifle battalions and a regiment of Cossacks in or near the town; while two batteries of artillery are, I believe, stationed further south, at Arman Sagait. Askabad is the residence of the Governor-General and Commander-in-Chief (the two functions in a military *régime* being united in the same individual), and the administrative centre of Transcaspia. The present Governor is General Komaroff, a man whose name is well known to Englishmen as the Russian commander in the famous affair on the Kushk, on March 30, 1885, which we have named from the contiguous and disputed district of Penjdeh. Into the question at issue between him and Sir Peter Lumsden I do not wish to re-enter. I afterwards met General Komaroff, and enjoyed an interesting conversation with him, to which I shall have occasion further to allude. He is a short, stout, middle-aged man, with a bald head, spectacles, and a square grizzled beard, and cannot be described as of dignified appearance. Indeed he reminded me of a university professor dressed up in uniform, and metamorphosed from a civilian into a soldier. To administrative energy he adds the tastes of a student and the enthusiasm of an antiquarian; having, as he informed me, amassed a collection of the antiquities of Transcaspia, including a statuette, apparently of Athene, of the best Greek period, some ornaments in the style of the beautiful Kertch collection at St. Petersburg, and no less than forty specimens of coins not previously known.

The Government of Transcaspia has, during the last five years, reached such dimensions that rumours have been heard of its approaching declaration of independence of the Caucasus, by the Governor-

General of which it is still controlled; while a short time ago General Komaroff is said to have defeated a scheme to render it subordinate to the Governor-General of Turkestan, hitherto the greatest potentate of Central Asia, and to have sought from the Emperor the privilege of responsibility to him alone. If subordination to the Caucasus is perpetuated, it will only be because of the easy and uninterrupted communication between Transcaspia and that part of the empire, in contrast to European Russia, and because in time of war the Caucasus would be the base from which reinforcements and supplies would naturally be drawn. If, on the other hand, it is placed under Turkestan, it will be because of the danger of divided military action in a region so critical as the Afghan border. In any case, the increasing importance of Transcaspia affords a striking illustration of a fact, to which I shall subsequently revert, viz. the shifting from east to west of the centre of gravity in the Central Asian dominions of the Czar, with its consequent bearings, of incalculable importance, upon the relations of Russia and Great Britain in the East.

Askabad itself has a printing-press, a photographic establishment, and European shops and hotels. The houses are for the most part of one storey, and are freely bedaubed with white. A small fortified *enceinte* supplies a reminder of the days, not yet ten years gone by, when the Russians were strangers and suspects in the land. In the centre of the town is an obelisk erected in memory of the artillerymen who were killed in the siege and capture of Geok Tepe, and at its base are planted the Afghan guns which were captured in the skirmish on the Kushk. The town is a purely Russian settlement, though the business quarter has attracted a large number of Armenians, Persians, and Jews. City life is avoided by the Turkomans, who prefer the tented liberty of the steppe.

Askabad is also a place of high strategical significance, as being the meeting-point of the Khivan and Persian roads. Already the north of Persia and Khorasan are pretty well at Russian mercy from a military point of view; though there is some bravado in talking, as the Russians always do, of the Shah as a vassal, and of Persia as in a parallel plight to Bokhara or Khiva. Since the occupation of Transcaspia the Russians have rendered an advance still more easy by constructing a military road from 20 ft. to 24 ft. broad, and available for artillery, from Askabad over the Kopet Dagh to the Persian frontier, where at present it terminates abruptly at one of the frontier pillars placed by the Commission near the hamlet of Baz Girha. The distance is thirty miles from Askabad. At present there is nothing better than a mountain track, descending upon the other side to Kuchan and the high road to Meshed; a contrast which is due to the failure of the Persians to fulfil their part of the bargain, Russia having undertaken to construct the first section of the *chaussée* to the frontier, while the remaining portion of forty miles to Kuchan was to be laid by General Gasteiger Khan for the Government of the Shah. To this co-operate roadway was to be joined a steam tramway originally projected by a merchant named Nikolaieff, which was to cover the remaining 100 miles to Meshed, and, under the guise of commercial transit, to provide Russia with a private way of entry into Khorasan. There is reason to believe that, elated with its recent successes in the matter of a Russian consul at Meshed, the Imperial Government is urgently pressing for the execution of this project; and at any moment we may find that the centre of interest has shifted from the Afghan to the Persian frontier. This is a question of which I shall have something to say later on. In any case, whether a future movement upon Khorasan be forcible or pacific, this road will without doubt afford the main and a most effective line of advance. Already it has been announced in the press that it is beginning to be used by Bokharan merchants, in connection with the caravan routes through Persia from the ports of Bender-Abbas or Bushire, for merchandise from India, in preference to the shorter but less safe and more costly routes through Afghanistan.

A politic act on the part of General Annenkoff was the issue of a proclamation pointing out the advantages of his railway, in connection with the Askabad-Kuchan road, to pilgrims of the Shiite persuasion, both from Western Persia and from the provinces of the Caucasus, desirous of reaching the sacred city of Meshed – advantages by which I was informed that they already profit in considerable numbers. Not that the orthodox Sunnite is without his equal consolations from the line. It is, in fact, becoming a popular method of locomotion, on the first part of the way to Mecca, for the devout *hadji* of Bokhara, Samarkand, and the still further east. Six thousand such pilgrims travelled upon it in 1887; and it was estimated that the total would reach ten thousand in 1888.

Among the stations passed after leaving Askabad are Gyaurs and Baba Durmaz, both of which were familiar names during the epoch when Russian diplomacy averred and British credulity believed that the limit of Russian advance could be drawn somewhere or anywhere between Askabad and Merv. The former is generally recognised as the commencement of the Atek or mountain-base oasis, in which horticulture and agriculture continue to prevail, and which is prolonged as far as the rich pastures of Sarakhs. The greater part of it was acquired by treaty with Persia in 1881. Artik, the next station to Baba Durmaz, is only a few miles from Lutfabad, a Persian town on the near side of the mountains, round which a loop was thrown, leaving it to Persia, in the delimitation that followed upon the treaty of that year. The oasis ends at Dushak, a place of considerable importance, inasmuch as it is the present southernmost station of the line, where the rails run nearest to Afghanistan, and the consequent starting-point for Sarakhs and the frontier at Zulfikar, from which it is distant only 130 miles. When any extension of the line in a southerly direction is contemplated – a subject of which I shall have more to say – it might possibly be from Dushak (a Persian name with the curiously apt signification of Two Branches) that it would start; and should the idea of an Indo-Russian railway ever emerge from the limbo of chimeras in which it is at present interned, it would be from Dushak that the lines of junction with Chaman, Quetta, and the Bolan would most naturally be laid.

Some of my friends on our return journey contemplated making a little

I should greatly like to have seen Kelat-i-Nadiri, visited, or mapped, or described by Colonel Valentine Baker.

excursion from Dushak over the Persian frontier to the native Khanate of Kelat-i-Nadiri and possibly even as far as Meshed, a distance over a very rough mountain road of eighty miles; but on telegraphing to the Russian authorities at Askabad for permission to pass the frontier and to return by the same route, we were peremptorily forbidden, the officer who dictated the despatch subsequently informing me that the frontier was not safe in these parts, a murder having recently been committed there or thereabouts, and that the consent of the Persian authorities would have had to be obtained from Teheran, as well as a special authorisation from St. Petersburg – an accumulation of excuses which was hardly wanted to explain the refusal of the Russians to allow three Englishmen to visit so tenderly nursed a region as the frontiers of Khorasan. Kelat, indeed, is understood to be the point of the Persian frontier where Russian influence, and, it is alleged, Russian roubles, are most assiduously at work; and where the troubles and risk of future conquest are being anticipated by the surer methods of subsidised conciliation.

I should greatly like to have seen Kelat-i-Nadiri, which is a most interesting place, and of which more will be heard in the future. Visited, or mapped, or described, by Sir C. MacGregor ("Journey through Khorasan"), Colonel Valentine Baker ("Clouds in the East"),

Tekke Chiefs of the Tejend which teems with wild fowl and game of every description, particularly wild boars.

O'Donovan ("The Merv Oasis"), and Captain A. C. Yate ("Travels with the Afghan Boundary Commission"), it is known to be one of the strongest natural fortresses in the world. An elevated valley of intensely fertile soil, irrigated by a perennial stream, is entirely surrounded and shut out from external communication by a lofty mountain barrier, from 800 to 1,200 feet high, with a precipitous scarp of from 300 to 600 feet. The cliffs are pierced by only five passages, which are strongly fortified and impregnable to attack. The entire enclosure, which O'Donovan very aptly compared with the Happy Valley of Rasselas, and which is a kingdom in miniature, is twenty-one miles long and from five to seven miles broad. Its value to Russia lies in its command of the head-waters of the streams that irrigate the Atek. In the spring of this year (April 1889) it was rumoured that Kelat had been ceded by Persia to Russia; but enquiries very happily proved that this was not the case.

From Dushak, where we finally lose sight of the great mountain wall, under the shadow of which we have continued so long, the railway turns at an angle towards the north-east and enters the Tejend oasis. Presently it crosses the river of that name, which is merely another title for the lower course of the Heri Rud, where it emerges from the mountains and meanders over the sandy plain (the oasis is a thing of the future rather than of the present) prior to losing itself in a marshy swamp in the Kara Kum. Among the rivers of this country, none present more striking contrasts, according to the season of the year, than the Tejend. At time of high water, in April and May, it has a depth of forty feet, and a width, in different parts, of from eighty yards to a quarter of a mile. Later on, under the evaporation of the summer heats, it shrinks to a narrow streamlet, or is utterly exhausted by irrigation canals. The Tejend swamp is overgrown by a sort of cane-brake or jungle teeming with wild fowl and game of every description, particularly wild boars. General Annenkoff's first bridge crosses the river at a point where it is from 80 to 100 yards wide. Then follow the sands again; for wherever water has not been conducted there is sand, and the meaning of an oasis in these parts is, as I have said, simply a steppe rendered amenable to culture by artificial irrigation, there being no reason why, if a more abundant water supply could either be manipulated or procured, the whole country should not in time, if I may coin the word, be oasified. The sands continue for nearly fifty miles, till we again find ourselves in the midst of life and verdure, and on the early morning of our second day after leaving the Caspian glide into a station bearing the historic name of Merv.

From Merv to the Oxus

But I have seen
Afrasiab's cities only, Samarkand,
Bokhara, and lone Khiva in the waste,
And the black Toorkmun tents; and only drunk
The desert rivers, Moorghub and Tejend,
Kohik, and where the Kalmuks feed their sheep,
The Northern Sir, and the great Oxus stream,
The yellow Oxus.

MATTHEW ARNOLD, *Sohrab and Rustum.*

WHEN O'Donovan rode into Merv on March 1, 1881, after following on horseback much the same route from the Persian frontier as we have been doing by rail, he confessed to a sense of disappointment at finding the domes and minarets of the great city of his imagination dwindle into a couple of hundred huts, placed on the right bank of a scanty stream. The visitor of today, who, though he be, thanks to O'Donovan and others, better informed, yet still expects some halo of splendour to linger round the ancient Queen of the World, suffers an almost similar disenchantment. He sees only a nascent and as yet very embryonic Russian town, with some station buildings, two or three streets of irregular wooden houses, and of generally inchoate appearance, and that is all. No ancient city, no ruins, no signs of former greatness or reviving prosperity. It is true that on the other side of the Murghab – at the season of the year when

A bridge over the Merv or Maour or Merou of which Moore sang.

I saw it a slender but very muddy stream, flowing in a deep bed between lofty banks, and here crossed by a wooden pile bridge, fifty-five yards long – he sees looming up the earthen walls of the unfinished fortress of Koushid Khan Kala, upon which the Mervi were so busily engaged during O'Donovan's stay in 1881. But these have to a large extent been pulled down or have fallen into decay; and the romance is not restored to them by the discovery that they now contain several unimpeachable whitewashed dwellings of European structure and appearance, which are in fact the Russian official quarters, and edifices, and comprise the residences of Colonel Alikhanoff, Governor of Merv, General Annen-koff, the colonel commanding the garrison, and others, as well as public gardens and a small Russian church. The fact is that this Merv never was an important city, or even a city at all. It is merely a site, first occupied by the Tekke Turkomans when under their famous leader Koushid Khan they swept up the valley of the Murghab in the year 1856, driving the Sariks or previous settlers before them, and ousting them from their city of Porsa Kala, the ruins of which still stand twenty miles to the south. Not that the Sarik city itself had any closer connection with the Merv of antiquity, the Merv or Maour or Merou of which Arab scribes wrote so lovingly, and of which Moore sang:

> And fairest of all streams the Murga roves
> Among Merou's bright palaces and groves.

The real and ancient Merv or Mervs – for there were three successive cities – are situated ten miles across the plain to the east, and will be mentioned later on.

It was only after the youngest of these was sacked at the end of the last century, and the irrigation works, upon which its life depended, were destroyed, that the Turkomans moved westwards and made the western branch of the Murghab their headquarters. Of a people who led so unsettled a life, and whose largest centre of population was not a city but a camp, it would be useless to expect any permanent relics; and therefore it is not surprising that the present Merv consists only of the rickety town which the Russians have built, and which is inhabited mainly by Persians, Jews, and Armenians, and of the official quarter before alluded to within the mouldering walls of the never-completed Tekke fortress. The town itself, so far from increasing, is at the present moment diminishing in numbers. A visitor in 1886 describes its population as 3,000; but it cannot now be more than one-third of that total. The reason of the diminution is this. From the time of the annexation in February, 1884, and while the railway was being pushed forward to Amu Daria, Merv was the headquarters of General Annenkoff and his staff. There was a sudden inflation of business, shops were run up, merchants came, and the brand-new Merv fancied that it had inherited some aroma of the ancient renown. A club-house, open, as the Russian military clubs always are, to both sexes, provided a centre of social reunion, and was the scene of weekly dancing and festivity. For the less select, a music-hall re-echoed on the banks of the Murghab the airs of Offenbach and the melodies of Strauss. The Turkomans, attracted by the foreign influx, flocked in large numbers from their settlements on the oasis, and drove an ephemeral but thriving trade. But with the forward movement of the railway battalion, and still more with the occupation by the line of Bokhara and Samarkand, this fictitious importance died away, most of the shops were shut, the town now contains only 285 houses, numbered from one upwards, and except on bazaar days, which are twice a week, and when a dwindling crowd of natives collects in the open air on the other or right bank of the Murghab, very little business appears to be done. Whether or not the glory of Merv may revive will depend upon the success or failure of the schemes for the regeneration of the surrounding oasis, which are now being undertaken.

Of the ancient history of Merv, it will be sufficient here to say that it has been one of even greater and more startling vicissitudes than are common with the capitals of the East. Its glories and sieges and sacks excited the eloquence of chroniclers and the wonderment of pilgrims. Successively, a satrapy of Darius (under the name Margush, whence obviously the Greek Margus (Murghab) and Margiana); a city and colony of Alexander; a province of the Parthians, whither Orodes transported the 10,000 Roman soldiers whom he took prisoners in his famous victory over Crassus; the site of a Christian bishopric; an Arabian capital (where, at the end of the eighth century, Mokannah, the veiled prophet of Khorasan, kindled the flame of schism); the seat of power of a Seljuk dynasty, and the residence and last resting-place of Alp Arslan and Sultan Sanjur; a prey to the awful scourge of the Mongol, and an altar for the human hecatombs of Jenghiz Khan; a frontier outpost of Persia; a bone of armed contention between Bokhara and Khiva; a Turkoman encampment; and a Russian town – it has surely exhausted every revolution of fortune's wheel, and in its last state has touched the expiring chord of the diapason of romance. For English travellers and readers, its interest lies less in the faded tomes of the past than in the records of the present century, during which several visits to it, or attempts to visit it, have been made by the small but heroic band of British pioneers in Central Asia.

Dr. Wolff, the missionary, was twice at Merv, in 1831 and again in 1844, upon his courageous errand of enquiry into the Stoddart and Conolly tragedy at Bokhara. Burnes halted on the Murghab, but did not see Merv itself, on his way from Bokhara to Meshed in 1832. Abbott and Shakespear were there in 1840 on their journey to Khiva. Thomson, in 1843, was the next, and Wolff was the last English visitor for nearly forty years; MacGregor and Burnaby being both recalled in 1875, when about to start for Merv, from the West and North respectively. At length, in 1881, the curtain of mystery, torn aside by the adventurous hand of O'Donovan, revealed the Tekke Turkoman clans existing under a tribal form of government, regulated by a council and presided over by khans, and debating with feverish anxiety the impending advance of the terrible "Ouroussi".

The circumstances of the later and pacific annexation of Merv are well known, having been debated in Parliament, discussed in Blue Books, and enshrined in substantial volumes. There can be no doubt that immediately after the victory of Geok Tepe the thoughts of the Russians were turned in the direction of Merv, and Skobeleff was bitterly disappointed at not being allowed to push on so far. Prudence, however, and still more the desirability of calming the suspicions of England, suggested a temporary delay, and the employment of more insidious means. Accordingly, commercial relations were opened with the inhabitants of the Merv oasis; surveys of their country, and even of their encampment, were obtained by Alikhanoff, who under the guise of a merchant's clerk accompanied a trading caravan thither in February 1882, and conducted secret negotiations with the more propitious chieftains; the rouble was plentifully distributed; and finally, in the spring of 1884 – while British hands were full in Upper Egypt and no untimely interference was to be expected – the same Alikhanoff, reappearing upon the scene, enforced, by significant allusions to a Russian detachment in the immediate neighbourhood, his demand for a surrender of the tribe and their oasis to the Czar. The chief acquiesced and took the oath of allegiance. Komaroff's troops advanced at full speed, before the Anti-Russian party, under the lead of Kadjar Khan and one Siakh-Push, an Afghan fanatic who seems to have exercised an extraordinary influence over the Tekkes, could organise a serious resistance. A few shots were exchanged, and a certain number of Turkoman saddles emptied; the fortress of Koushid Khan Kala was occupied, the hostile leaders fled or were captured; a shower of stars and medals from St. Petersburg rewarded the services of conquest or sweetened the pains of surrender; and Merv was at last made part and parcel of the Russian Empire. The flame of diplomatic protest blazed fiercely forth in England; but, after a momentary combustion, was, as usual, extinguished by a flood of excuses from the inexhaustible reservoirs of the Neva.

The oasis of Merv, which owes its existence to the bounty of the river Murghab and its subsidiary network of canals and streams, is said in most works on the subject to consist of about 1,600 square miles; though at present but a small fraction of this extent is under systematic or scientific cultivation. Its natural fertility is greater by far than that of any of the three oases hitherto encountered. As early as the tenth century the Arab traveller, Ibn Haukal, affirmed that "the fruits of Merv are finer than those of any other place, and in no other city are to be seen such palaces and groves, and gardens and streams." Vanished, alas! is all this ancient splendour; but still the cattle of its pastures, the fruits of its orchards – grapes, peaches, apricots, and mulberries – and the products of its fields – wheat, cotton, barley, sorghum, sesame, rice, and melons, yielding from twenty-fold to one hundred-fold – are superior to those of any other district between Khiva and Khorasan. Linked to it in a chain of fertilised tracts towards the south and south-west are the minor oases of Yuletan, Sarakhs, and Penjdeh, inhabited by the Sarik and Salor Turkomans, living in scattered encampments or *aouls*.

In speaking of the Merv oasis, I am referring to that which is still in a backward condition, and is capable of immense development. The soil is well adapted to the growth of cotton, though little is at present produced, the Turkomans apparently not having taken very kindly to the industry, though after the Russian occupation several tons of American cotton-seed were distributed gratis among the inhabitants. Here, however, as well as along the equally suitable banks of the Oxus, improvement may be expected. The growth of timber, so necessary in these parched regions, has also been taken in hand. General Komaroff told me that the planting of the oasis had been commenced in real earnest, and that in time there would be growing there not less than sixty million of trees. Three million young saplings were already to be seen at the height of several feet from the ground at Bairam Ali, ten miles to the east. At the same time the work of scientific irrigation, hitherto neglected, has been begun – the repair of the great Sultan Bend Dam, fifty-three miles further up the course of the Murghab, by which alone its distribution over the lower surfaces can be properly regulated, having been committed to a young Polish engineer named Poklefski, and the entire district having been made over to the private purse of the Czar – a guarantee that its development will not be allowed to slacken, or its revenues to result in loss to the exchequer of so economical a monarch. When the new system of canalisation is in working order, it is anticipated that it will subdue to cultivation a territory of some 200,000 acres, upon which it is proposed to plant Russian peasants as colonists in equal number with the Turkomans. If we add to this that Merv is the very central point of the trade routes from Bokhara and the Oxus to Eastern Persia, and from Central Asia to India through Afghanistan, we can believe that there yet may rise on the banks of the Murghab a city worthy of the site and of the name.

When Alikhanoff, in the disguise of a clerk, visited Merv in 1882, his report to the Russian Government contained the following not too flattering account of his future subjects: "Besides being cruel, the Merv Tekkes never keep a promise or an oath if it suits their purpose to break it. In addition to this they are liars and gluttons. They are frightfully envious; and finally, among all the Turkomans there is not a people so unattractive in every moral respect as the Tekkes of Merv." We may conjecture that this is a verdict which he would not now endorse without qualification; and though the broad features of the national character may remain stereotyped – though Turkoman morals are indubitably coarse, and their standards of honesty low, yet later travellers who have resided in their midst, or have had occasion to employ their services, have testified to the possession of good qualities on their part, such as amiability, frankness, hospitality, and a rough code of honour. M. Bonvalot, the French traveller, who was at Merv in 1886, wrote a letter to the *Journal des Débats*, in which he said, "The Russians are of opinion, and I agree with them, that the Tekkes are worthy people, very affable and mild, and with a frankness that is both astonishing and delightful after the rascality of the Persians and the platitudes of the Bokhariots." Their behaviour is largely dependent upon the handling of the Russians, which has so far been

There is not a people so unattractive in every moral respect as the Tekkes of Merv.

eminently successful. As the same authority very truly remarked in his latest work, "So long as they can get water, toleration, speedy, stern and equitable justice, and have their taxes levied fairly, the people of Central Asia do not as a rule ask for anything more."

The overwhelming strategical importance of Merv in relation to India is a dictum which I have never been able to understand. I have seen it argued with irreproachable logic, in magazine articles, that Merv is the key to Herat, Herat the key to Kandahar, and Kandahar the key to India. But the most scientific demonstrations of *a priori* reasoning must after all yield place to experience and to fact. Russia holds Merv; and she could tomorrow, if she chose to bring about a war with England, seize Herat; not, however, because she holds Merv, but because she holds the far more advanced and important positions of Sarakhs and Penjdeh. But even if she held Herat she would not therefore imperil Kandahar, while even if she held both Herat and Kandahar, she would not be much nearer the conquest of India. A great deal of nonsense has been talked in England about these so-called keys to India, and Lord Beaconsfield never said a truer thing, though at the time it was laughed at as a sounding platitude, than when he declared that the keys of India are to be found in London, and consist in the spirit and determination of the British people. The political benefits to Russia resulting from the annexation of Merv were very considerable, and ought not to be underrated. They were threefold, having an easterly, a westerly, and a local application. It set the seal upon the absorption of the Khanates, by establishing Russia upon the left as well as upon the right of Bokhara, and leaving that country very much in the position of metal between the hammer and the anvil, to be moulded or flattened at will. It completed the flank circumvention of Khorasan, by the erection of a powerful military post on its eastern or Afghan quarter. And finally it rounded off the conquest, and centralised the administration of the Turkoman oases and deserts, the bulk of which passed straightway, and the residue of which will ultimately pass, beneath Russian rule. Nor is the immediate value of Merv to Russia by any means to be despised, both because of its trading position, and because, being the centre of a large oasis, it could sustain a numerous army at a distance from its base through one or more winters. These are advantages on her side which it would be foolish to ignore, but which it is still more foolish to magnify into a real peril to our Indian possessions.

When we reached Merv I had hoped to find Colonel Alikhanoff, the celebrated governor of the district, to whom I had a letter of introduction. But he was absent, and the most mysterious and conflicting rumours prevailed as to his whereabouts. I ascertained afterwards, however, that he had left suddenly for the frontier with a Russian battalion and a squadron of the Turkoman cavalry; and the fact that a Cossack officer, travelling in our company to rejoin his regiment at Merv, was abruptly ordered to follow in the same direction showed that something was on the *tapis* in that quarter. I mentioned in my first chapter that the revolt of Is-hak Khan in Afghanistan had been alleged in St. Petersburg as a reasonable excuse for the prohibition of our journey to Transcaspia; and I had been much interested at reading in the Russian journals, which are, as is well known, subject to official supervision, the most exaggerated and fantastic estimates of the Afghan Pretender's chances of success. These reports were so absurdly biased as to leave no doubt, not merely that Is-hak Khan had the clandestine sympathy of the Russian Government, but that he was publicly regarded as the Russian candidate to the Afghan throne. Upon arriving at Merv we heard a rumour that Abdurrahman was dead, and that Is-hak, who had been uniformly successful, was marching upon Kabul. This single item of false information will give some idea of the inferiority under which Russia seems to labour as compared with ourselves in point of news from Afghanistan. Her intelligence comes in the main via Balkh and the Oxus to Bokhara, and appears to be as unreliable as is the news from Bokhara commonly transmitted to the British Government through Stamboul. However, this news, false though it was, had been enough to throw the Russian military authorities into a ferment; and what I afterwards heard at Tashkent made it clear that there was a considerable massing of Russian troops upon the Afghan frontier, and that a forward movement must even have been contemplated. I asked a Russian diplomatist what excuse his country could possibly have for interfering in Afghanistan at this juncture, even if Is-hak Khan were successful; and he wisely professed an ignorance on the subject equal to my own. But the fact remains that the troops were so moved, and that at Kerki, the Russian frontier station on the Amu Daria, there was collected at this time a body of men, enormously in excess of garrison requirements, and therefore of threatening dimensions. In Tashkent I was informed by an officer that the talk was all of an invasion of Afghanistan and of war; and though I do not desire to attach any importance to the military gossip of a place where bellicose ideas have always prevailed, and where there is no lack of spirits who care little about morality, but a great deal about medals – still I must place on record the fact that, in a time of absolute peace and with no possible provocation, the Russians considered themselves sufficiently interested in the internal status of Afghanistan, a country which they have a score of times declared to be outside the sphere of their legitimate political interference, to make a menacing display of military force upon her frontier.

There was not at that time the provocation which the Amir Abdurrahman is since alleged to have given by the ferment arising out of his vindictive punishment of the rebels and suspects in Afghan Turkestan, and which was followed in February of this year by much larger Russian concentration on the boundary. In neither case was any legitimate excuse likely to be forthcoming for advance. For in the former instance the success of Is-hak Khan would not have justified a violation of the frontier by Russia, any more than his defeat was likely to lead to its violation by Afghanistan; whilst in the latter, the proceedings of Abdurrahman, though perhaps well calculated to cause a great local stir, admitted of no aggressive interpretation as regards either Russia or Bokhara, into whose territories so calculating a ruler was not in the least likely to rush to his own perdition. The Russian movements on both occasions, if they illustrate nothing more, are at least noteworthy as testifying to the anxiety with which they regard the Oxus frontier, and to the watchful, if not covetous, eye which they direct upon Afghan Turkestan. Though the war-cloud has for the present happily rolled by in that quarter, we must not be surprised if before long its horrid shadow reappears. When I afterwards heard at Tashkent of the collapse of Is-hak, the rumour prevailed that he had fled to Bokhara, and from there had been removed to his old quarters at Samarkand. This last report was denied by the Russian officials, who repudiated any desire to countenance the pretender by allowing him an asylum on Russian soil. A significant commentary on their denial was afforded by his subsequent retreat at their invitation to that very spot, where he now resides surrounded by a considerable retinue, a tool in the hands of his hosts, and whom we may expect at any moment to see re-emerge as a thorn in our side, in the event either of disaster or of death to Abdurrahman Khan.

I subsequently met Colonel Alikhanoff and was introduced to him by General Komaroff. Speaking of the aptitude which Russia has so often displayed for employing in her own armies those whom she has already vanquished as opponents, the general told me that Alikhanoff's father, who was now a general, had himself fought against Russia in the Caucasian wars. This provoked the obvious rejoinder, that the way to become a Russian general was clearly to begin by having been a Russian foe. Of the personality of Alikhanoff himself I believe that a somewhat mistaken impression exists in England. Those who are acquainted with the part that he played in the diplomatic subjugation of Merv between the years 1882 and 1884, to which I have already alluded, or who have read of his great influence in the Turkoman oasis, and of his Mussulman religion, are apt to picture to themselves a man of Oriental habits and appearance. A greater mistake could not be made. Alikhanoff is a tall man, with ruddy complexion, light hair, and a prodigious auburn, almost reddish, beard. A Lesghian of Daghestan by birth, whose real name is Ali Khan Avarski, he has all the appearance of having hailed from the banks of the Tay or the Clyde. He has been in the Russian army from early years, and served under Skobeleff in the Khivan campaign. Already a major, he was degraded to the ranks in 1875 because of a duel with a brother officer, and served as a private in the Russo-Turkish war. When the Turkoman expeditions began in 1879, he went to Asia, reached the highest non-commissioned officer's rank in the same year, and returned at the close of Skobeleff's campaign in 1881. Promoted a captain after his reconnaissance of the Merv oasis in 1882, and a major after the annexation of Merv in 1884, he is now a full colonel in the Russian army, Nachalnik or Governor of the Merv oasis, Warden of the Marches along the Afghan border, and judge of appeal among the Turkoman tribes, and at the early age of forty, though reported to be a dissatisfied man, finds himself the most talked of personage in Central Asia. His religion, no doubt, stands him in great stead. But I do not know what other special advantages he possesses beyond his own ability and courage.

As the central point between Turkestan and Transcaspia and as commanding the Russo-Afghan frontier, Merv is an important garrison town. According to the latest information, there are stationed here two battalions of the line, a regiment of Cossacks, a battery of artillery, and a company of sappers.

Although the Turkoman force is at present limited to 300 men, it may be regarded as being reinforced by a powerful unmobilised reserve. Nearly every Turkoman who can afford it keeps a horse, and, unable to play the freebooter, is quite ready to turn free lance at a moment's notice. General Komaroff assured me that the total under arms could without difficulty be increased to 8,000, and I afterwards read in the *Times* that Colonel Alikhanoff told the correspondent of that paper that in twenty-four hours he could raise 6,000 mounted men – a statement which tallies with that of the general. If there is some exaggeration in these estimates, at least there was no want of explicitness in the famous threat of Skobeleff, who in his memorandum on the invasion of India, drawn up in 1877, wrote: "It will be in the end our duty to organise masses of Asiatic cavalry and to hurl them into India as a vanguard, under the banner of blood and rapine, thereby reviving the times of Tamerlane." Even if this sanguinary forecast be forgotten, or if it remain unrealised, there is yet sound

The total under arms could without difficulty be increased to 8,000.

129

policy in this utilisation of the Turkoman manhood, inasmuch as it may operate as an antidote to the deteriorating influence of European civilisation, which, entering this unsophisticated region in its own peculiar guise, and bringing brandy and *vodka* in its train, is already beginning to enfeeble the virile type of these former slave-hunters of the desert.

When General Grodekoff rode from Samarkand to Herat in 1878, he recorded his judgment of the value of the Turkoman horses in these words: "If ever we conquer Merv, besides imposing a money contribution, we ought to take from the Tekkes all their best stallions and mares. They would then at once cease to be formidable." For the policy of confiscation has wisely been substituted that of utilising the equine resources of the oasis. None the less it is open to question whether the power and endurance of the Turkoman horses, reputed though they are to be able to accomplish from 70 to 100 miles a day for a week at a time, have not been greatly exaggerated. Travellers have related astonishing stories second-hand of their achievements; but those who have had actual experience are content with a more modest tale. Certainly the long neck, large head, narrow chest, and weedy legs of the Turkoman horse do not correspond with European taste in horseflesh. But the English members of the Afghan Boundary Commission thought still less of them in use. A few only were bought at prices of from 20l. to 25l. And Colonel Ridgeway, who was authorised by the Indian Government to expend 300l.

Nearly every Turkoman who can afford it keeps a horse.

upon first-class Turkoman stallions for breeding purposes, did not draw one penny upon his credit.

It was with perfect justice that General Komaroff boasted of the facility with which Russia succeeds in enlisting, not only the services, but the loyalty of her former opponents. The volunteer enrolment of the Turkoman horse would be a sufficient proof of this, had it not already been paralleled in India and elsewhere. But I can give a more striking illustration still. On my return to Baku, I saw drawn up on the landing-stage to greet the Governor-General a number of gorgeously-clad Turkomans, robed in magnificent velvet or embroidered *khalats*, and their breasts ablaze with decorations. They, too, had come over to be presented to the Czar. At the head of the line stood a dignified-looking Turkoman, with an immense pair of silver epaulettes on his shoulders. This, the general told me, was Makdum Kuli Khan, son of the famous Tekke chieftain Nur Verdi Khan by an Akhal wife, the hereditary leader of the Vekhil or Eastern division of the Merv Tekkes, and the chief of the Akhal Tekkes in Geok Tepe at the time of the siege. Reconciled to Russia at an early date, he was taken to Moscow to attend the coronation of the Czar in 1883, and is now a full colonel and Governor of the Tejend oasis – where but lately, in the exercise of his administrative powers, he, a Turkoman and an old Russian enemy, arrested a Russian captain serving under his command. And yet this was the man who, in 1881, told

The Khans of Merv, only eight years ago the bitter and determined enemies of Russia.

Edmund O'Donovan that "it was the intention of himself and his staunch followers to fight to the last should Merv be invaded by the Russians, and if beaten to retire into Afghanistan. If not well received there, they purposed asking an asylum within the frontiers of British India." Adjoining him stood his younger brother, Yussuf Khan, son of Nur Verdi by his famous Merv wife, Gur Jemal, a boy of fifteen or sixteen at the time of O'Donovan's visit, but now a Russian captain; Maili Khan and Sari Batir Khan, chiefs of the Sichmaz and Bakshi, two others of the four tribes of Merv; old Murad Bey, leader of the Beg subdivision of the Toktamish clan, who conducted O'Donovan to the final meeting of the Great Council; and, mirabile dictu, Baba Khan himself, son of the old conqueror Koushid Khan, and hereditary leader of the Toktamish, the one-eyed Baba, who led the English party at Merv in 1881, and, in order to demonstrate his allegiance to the Queen, branded his horses with V.R. reversed and imprinted upside down. The three last-named are now majors in the Russian service. Baba's colleague of the Triumvirate of 1881, Niaz Khan, is also a Russian officer, but did not appear to be present. The old Ikhtyar at the date of O'Donovan's arrival, Kadjar Khan, who led the forlorn anti-Russian movement in 1884, is detained in St. Petersburg. Gur Jemal, the elderly matron and former chieftainess, of whom I have spoken, and whose potent influence was so diplomatically enlisted by Russia prior to the annexation of Merv, was also in Baku, waiting to receive the compliments, to which she was unquestionably entitled, from the lips of the Emperor. There were also present the Khans of the Sarik and Salor Turkomans of Yuletan, Sarakhs, and Penjdeh, and some imposing Kirghiz notabilities with gorgeous accoutrements and prodigiously high steeple-crowned hats. The delegation brought with them rich carpets and a collection of wild animals as presents to the Emperor, who in return loaded them with European gifts and arms, and said in the course of his speech that he hoped to repay their visit at Merv in 1889 or 1890.

I do not think that any sight could have impressed me more profoundly with the completeness of Russia's conquest, or with her remarkable talents of fraternisation with the conquered, than the spectacle of these men (and among their thirty odd companions who were assembled with them, there were doubtless other cases as remarkable), only eight years ago the bitter and determined enemies of Russia on the battlefield, but now wearing her uniform, standing high in her service, and crossing to Europe in order to salute as their sovereign the Great White Czar. Skobeleff's policy of "Hands all round", when the fight is over, seems to have been not one whit less successful than was the ferocious severity of the preliminary blow.

If other evidence were needed of Russia's triumph, it might be found in the walls of the great earthen fortress of Koushid Khan Kala, through which the locomotive steams immediately after leaving the station at Merv. Erected in 1881 by forced labour, 8,000 Tekkes being daily engaged upon the enterprise, its unfinished and dismantled ramparts are not less eloquent in their testimony than was the shattered embankment

The great earthen fortresses of Koushid Khan Kala in their premature decay are imposing monuments of a bloodless victory (top).

Bairam Ali, in the midst of an absolute wilderness of crumbling brick and clay, the centre of bygone greatness (bottom).

of Geok Tepe. Sixty feet at their base, and twenty feet at the summit, and from thirty to forty feet high, and originally enclosing a space one and three-quarters of a mile long by three-quarters of a mile broad, these huge clay structures, which were intended finally and utterly to repel the Muscovite advance, have never either sheltered, besieged or withstood besiegers. Like a great railway embankment they overtop the plain, and in their premature decay are imposing monuments of a bloodless victory.

The military and political questions arising out of the mention of Merv have almost tempted me to forget my undertaking to make some allusion to the old cities that at different times have borne the name. When the train, however, after traversing the oasis for ten miles from the modern town, pulls up at the station of Bairam Ali, in the midst of an absolute wilderness of crumbling brick and clay, the spectacle of walls, towers, ramparts, and domes, stretching in bewildering confusion to the horizon, reminds us that we are in the centre of bygone greatness. Here, within a short distance of each other, and covering an area of several square miles, in which there is scarcely a yard without some remains of the past, or with a single perfect relic, are to be seen the ruins of at least three cities that have been born, and flourished, and have died. The eldest and easternmost of these is the city now called Giaour Kala, and variously attributed by the natives, according to the quality of their erudition, to Zoroaster, or to Iskander, the local name for Alexander the Great. In these parts anything old, and misty, and uncertain is set down with unfaltering confidence to the Macedonian conqueror.

The ubiquity and vitality of the Alexandrine legend is well illustrated by the story, told by the Russian traveller Pashino, of an Afghan whom he met in a train in India in 1875, and who, in reply to the information that the reigning emperor of Russia was Alexander, or Iskander, by name, exclaimed: "Dear me! was it not he who conquered India, and of whom a great deal is said in the Scriptures?"

I was told by a long resident in the country that the general knowledge of past history is limited to three names – Alexander, Tamerlane, and Kaufmann; the Russian Governor-General, as the most recent, being popularly regarded as the biggest personage of the three. Giaour Kala, if it be the city of Alexander, is the fort said to have been built by him in B.C. 328, on his return from the campaign in Sogdiana. It was destroyed by the Arabs 1,200 years ago. In its present state it consists of a great rectangular walled enclosure with the ruins of a citadel in its north-east corner. Next in age and size comes the city of the Seljuks, of Alp Arslan, the Great Lion, and of Sultan Sanjur, so celebrated in chronicles and legends, who in the twelfth century ruled as lieutenant of the Khalif in the almost independent kingdom of Khorasan. Pillaged and destroyed with true Mongol ferocity by the son of Jenghiz Khan about 1220, it now consists of a heap of shapeless ruins, above which loom the still intact dome and crumbling walls of the tomb of the great Sultan himself. The sepulchre of Alp Arslan with its famous inscription – "All ye who have seen the glory of Alp Arslan exalted to the heavens, come hither to Merv, and behold it buried in the dust" – has long disappeared, gravestone as

The still intact dome and crumbling walls of the tomb of the great Sultan himself.

well as glory having perished in the same ruin. Thirdly comes the Persian city of Bairam Ali, from which the station on the new railway is named, and which took its own name from its last defender and Khan, who perished 100 years ago while resisting the successful assault of Amir Maasum, otherwise known as Begi Jan or Shah Murad, of Bokhara. This was the final and last end of a real and visible Merv, which has since that date been a geographical designation instead of a built town. Very decrepit and sorrowful looked these wasting walls of sun-dried clay, these broken arches and tottering towers; but there is magnificence in their very extent, and a voice in the sorrowful squalor of their ruin. Prior to O'Donovan, Abbott was the only visitor who appears to have bestowed upon them the slightest attention. Excavations have never yet been properly undertaken on this interesting site, the Russians appearing to be too much occupied with the political settlement of the country to be able to turn a thought to archaeology or to research. But if history is of any account, a lucrative harvest ought here to await the excavator's spade.

Travelling thus Eastward, and arrested at each forward step by some relic of a dead civilisation, or of a glorious but forgotten past, the imagination of the European cannot but be impressed with the thought that he is mounting the stream of the ages, and tracing towards its remote source the ancestry from which his own race has sprung. His feet are treading in an inverse direction the long route of humanity. The train that hurries him onward into new scenes seems at the same time to carry him backward into antiquity, and with every league that he advances the *mise en scène* recedes into a dimmer distance. History lies outspread before him like the page of a Chinese manuscript, to decipher which he must begin at the bottom and work his way upwards to the top. Wherever he halts, there in a waste of ruin he discovers the flotsam and jetsam of the mighty human current that rolled down from the Central Asian plateau on to the plains of Europe and the shores of the Mediterranean. How eloquent is this dried-up river-bed, with its huge water-worn boulders lying as they were thrown up by the eddies of the vanished swirl! At last in our time the current would seem to have turned back upon itself, and man, like water, is following a law of nature in rising to his original level. His face is turned Eastward and he seeks his primaeval home.

In these solitudes, moreover, the traveller may realise in all its sweep the mingled gloom and grandeur of Central Asian scenery. Throughout the still night the fire-horse, as the natives have sometimes christened it, races onward, panting audibly, gutturally, and shaking a mane of sparks and smoke. Itself and its riders are all alone. No token or sound of life greets eye or ear; no outline redeems the level sameness of the dim horizon; no shadows fall upon the staring plain. The moon shines with dreary coldness from the hollow dome, and a profound and tearful solitude seems to brood over the desert. The returning sunlight scarcely dissipates the impression of sadness, of desolate and hopeless decay, of a continent and life sunk in a mortal swoon. The traveller feels like a wanderer at night in some desecrated graveyard, amid crumbling tombstones and half-obliterated mounds. A cemetery, not of hundreds of years but of thousands, not of families or tribes but of nations and empires, lies outspread around him; and ever and anon, in falling tower or shattered arch, he stumbles upon some poor unearthed skeleton of the past.

The Merv oasis is considered to extend for forty-five miles east from the bank of the Murghab, and for the greater part of this distance is well worthy of the name. Here I saw greater cultivation, a richer growth, and a more numerous native population than at any previous stage of the journey. The *ariks* or irrigation-channels still contained water, the infiltration of which accounted for the rich *parterres* of green. In and near the ditches grew tall plumed grasses five feet or six feet high. The native huts, clustered together like black beehives, showed that the Mervi had not under their new masters deserted their old habitations. The men were to be seen everywhere in the fields, lazily mounted on horses or on asses. When the desert reappears, it comes in the literal sense of the word with a vengeance. Between the oasis and the Amu Daria intervene a hundred miles of the sorriest waste that ever met the human eye. East and west, and north and south, stretches a troubled sea of sand, each billow clearly defined and arrested as it were in mid-career, like an ocean wave curving to fall. I never saw anything more melancholy than the appearance of this wilderness, and its sickle-shaped dome-like ridges of driven sand with smoky summits, succeeding each other with the regularity of infantry files. Each has the appearance of being cloven through the crown, the

side facing towards the north-east, whence the prevailing winds blow, being uniformly convex and smooth, while the southern face is vertical and abrupt. From time immemorial nature's curse has been upon this spot; and successive travellers and historians have testified to the dismal continuity of its reputation.

This was the most difficult section of the line to build, there being next to no natural vegetation to aid in fixing the sands, and the displacement when gales blew being tremendous. I have mentioned that the Russians are now in some places beginning to plant the *saxaoul*. This is a slight atonement for the foolish economy which led them, on their first arrival, almost to exterminate it in several districts for the sake of fuel. A relic of this mistaken policy in the shape of big stacks of gnarled roots and boughs may still be seen at several of the stations, which in this region are little more than rude shanties built of a few planks and half-buried in the sand. I expect that if General Annenkoff begins to expend his credit in this horrible waste, the major part will be swallowed up before he emerges on the other side.

At last, after a whole day of this desolation, we again come to cultivated land separated by a line that might have been drawn by a rule from the Kara Kum. Passing at a slight distance the town and fort of Tcharjui, where Bokharan territory begins, and which is commanded by a Beg or native Governor, the railway traverses six miles of orchard and garden and brings us at length to the source and giver of this great bounty, the

Fort of Tcharjui where Bokharan territory begins and which is commanded by a Beg or native Governor.

Amu Daria or Oxus itself. There in the moonlight gleamed before us the broad bosom of the mighty river that from the glaciers of the Pamir rolls its 1,500 miles of current down to the Aral Sea. In my ears were continually ringing the beautiful words of Matthew Arnold, who alone of English poets has made the great Central Asian river the theme of his muse, and has realised its extraordinary and mysterious personality. Just as when upon its sandy marge the hero Rustum bewailed his dead son, so now before our eyes

> the majestic river floated on
> Out of the mist and hum of that low land
> Into the frosty twilight, and there moved
> Rejoicing through the hushed Chorasmian waste
> Under the solitary moon.

The Gihon of Eden, "that encompasseth the whole land of Ethiopia" (Genesis ii.13.), the Vak-shu of Sanskrit literature, the Oxus of the Greeks, the Amu Daria, or River-Sea, of the Tartars – no river, not even the Nile, can claim a nobler tradition, or a more illustrious history. Descending from the hidden "Roof of the world", its waters tell of forgotten peoples and whisper secrets of unknown lands. They are believed to have rocked the cradle of our race. Long the legendary watermark between Iran and Turan, they have worn a channel deep into the fate of humanity. World-wide conquerors, an Alexander and a Tamerlane, slaked their horses' thirst in the Oxus stream; Eastern poets drank inspiration from its fountains; Arab geographers boasted of it as "superior in volume, in depth, and in breadth to all the rivers of the earth".

The bed of the Amu Daria – *i.e.* the depression which is covered in time of high water – is here between two and three miles wide; though in summer, when swollen by the melted snows of the Hindu Kush and the Pamir, the inundated surface sometimes extends to five miles. In the autumn and winter, when the waters have shrunk, the channel is confined within its true banks, and is then from half a mile to a mile in width, flowing with a rapid current of most irregular depth over a shifting and sandy bottom. When Burnes crossed it at Tcharjui in August 1832, he found the channel about 650 yards across. At the time of our visit, in October 1888, the stream was unusually low, and the main channel was of no greater dimensions. Mud-banks, covered with ooze or sand, showed where the current had only recently subsided. Still, however, did it merit the title, "The great Oxus stream, the yellow Oxus". The colour of the water is a very dirty coffee-hued brown, the facsimile of that of the Nile; but it is extremely healthy and can be drunk with impunity. I was strangely reminded by the appearance of this great river, by the formation of its bed, by the structure of its banks, and by the scenery and life which they displayed, of many a landscape on the Nile in Upper Egypt. There is the same fringe of intensely fertile soil along its shores, with the same crouching clay-built villages, and even a Bokharan counterpart to the *sakkiyeh* and *shadoof*, for raising and distributing the life-giving

waters of the stream. Only on the Oxus there is no cliff like the eastern wall of the Nile at Gebel-et-Tayr, and, alas! in this northern latitude there is no belt of coroneted palms.

General Annenkoff's bridge is looked upon by his followers with parental pride.

The problem of crossing the Amu Daria at this place was regarded as the most serious difficulty by which General Annenkoff was confronted, and the bridge by which he solved it, though confessedly only a temporary structure, is looked upon by his followers with parental pride. It is an inelegant structure, built entirely of wood, which was brought all the way from Russia, and rests on more than 3,000 piles, which are driven very close together into the bed of the stream. At first the plan was contemplated of conveying the railway across upon a kind of steam ferry worked by a cable which was to be fixed upon a largish island in mid-stream. But this idea was presently surrendered in favour of the existing structure, which was designed by M. Daragan and built by a Polish engineer, named Bielinski, for the very moderate sum of £30,000, the economy of the undertaking being its chief recommendation to the authorities. It is constructed in four sections, there being four branches of the river at this spot, separated by islands. The united length of the four bridges is over 2,000 yards. M. Mestcherin told me with pride that the main part had been put up in the extraordinarily brief period of 103 days. The top of the bridge is inconsiderably elevated above the river, and the rails, though thirty feet above the lowest water, are only five feet above the level of the highest flood. A small plank platform and handrail runs alongside of the single line of rails. Our train crawled very slowly across, and occupied fifteen minutes in the transit.

As soon as the bridge was finished, the Russians with amazing stupidity did their best to ruin it altogether by cutting it in two. A section in the centre had been so constructed as to swing open and to admit of a steamboat, which had been built in St. Petersburg and put together just below, and in which it was expected that General Rosenbach, who came down to attend the inaugural function, would make a journey up-stream to Kerki. It did not seem to have occurred to anybody that if the steamer was only intended for up-stream traffic, it might as well have been pieced together above the bridge as below. However, when it approached the gap, this was discovered to have been made just too small. Sooner than disappoint the general, who was kept in ignorance of what was passing, or confess their blunder, the Russian engineers sliced another section of the bridge in two, pulling up two of the main clusters of piles. The result was that the bridge, frail enough to start with, and with its continuity thus cruelly shattered, nearly collapsed altogether; and some months were spent in getting it into working order again. It was quite anticipated that it would not survive the unusually high floods of 1888; and no one believes it can last more than a very few years. An even greater risk, to which so prodigious a structure built entirely of wood is by its nature exposed, is that of fire, ignited by a falling spark. To meet this danger, six fire stations with pumps and hose have been established on the top. However, the bridge will already have served its purpose, if only in conveying across the material for the continuation of the railway to Samarkand, and must ultimately be replaced by a more solid iron fabric, the cost of which, according to the plan of construction, is variously estimated at from £250,000 to £2,000,000 sterling. There is only one argument, apart from the cost, against an iron bridge, which may retard the execution. The Oxus is inclined to shift, not only its bed, but its entire channel. Tcharjui, now six miles inland, was originally upon the western bank of the river, and there cannot be a doubt that, whether it be due, as is said, to a centrifugal force arising from the rotation of the earth and compelling rivers to impinge upon their eastern banks, or to other causes, the eastward movement of the river still continues. It would be, to say the least, exasperating to build a big iron bridge to cross a river, and to find it eventually straddling over dry land. Training walls and a great expense would be required to counteract this danger.

Below the present bridge were to be seen some of the boats belonging to the much-vaunted Oxus flotilla, so dear to the imagination of Russian Jingoes, as providing a parallel line of advance upon Afghanistan. As yet its resources cannot be described as in a very forward condition as they consist of five vessels. It is evident that the Oxus flotilla, whose strength has been exaggerated in this country, is still in its infancy; and that, to whatever dimensions it may swell in the future, it cannot at present be looked upon as contributing much to the offensive strength of Russia in Central Asia.

Bokhara the Noble

Quant il orent passé cel desert, si vindrent à une cité qui est appelée Bocara, moult noble et grant. MARCO POLO.

I OBSERVED in the last chapter that, upon arriving at Tcharjui, we had passed from Russian on to Bokharan territory. The distinction is of course a somewhat artificial one, for though it rests upon treaty stipulations, yet Russia can do in Bokhara what she pleases, and when she humours the pretensions of Bokharan autonomy, only does so because, being all-powerful, she can afford to be lenient. The pretence of independence was, however, kept up, so far as the construction of the railway through the territory of the Amir was concerned – the strip of country traversed by the line and the ground occupied by the station buildings being in some cases presented gratis by the goodwill of the Amir, but in the majority of instances bought either from him or from the local proprietors of the soil. At that time Russian influence and credit do not appear to have been quite as omnipotent in Bokhara as they now are; for the Oriental landlords, with characteristic caution, turned up their noses at the paper rouble, and insisted upon being paid in silver, which had to be bought for the purpose in Hamburg, and transported all the way to Central Asia. I do not know whether the hypothesis of a similar transaction may be held to have explained the big padlocked bags, strongly guarded by soldiers, and evidently containing bullion, that I saw landed from our steamer at Uzun Ada.

As we advanced further into the Khanate, a new country spread before us. It displayed the exuberant richness, not merely of an oasis or reclaimed desert, but of a region long and habitually fertile. Great clumps of timber afforded a spectacle unseen since the Caucasus; and large walled enclosures, overtopped with fruit-trees, marked the country residences of Bokharan squires. It was of this neighbourhood that Ibn Haukal, the Arab traveller, wrote as long ago as the tenth century: "In all the regions of the earth there is not a more flourishing or a more delightful country than this, especially the district of Bokhara. If a person stand on the Kohendiz (*i.e.* the Castle) of Bokhara, and cast his eyes around, he shall not see anything but beautiful green and luxuriant verdure on every side; so that he would imagine the green of the earth and the azure of the heavens were united. And as there are green fields in every quarter, so there are villas interspersed among the green fields. And in all Khorasan and Maweralnahr there are not any people more long-lived than those of Bokhara." At Kara Kul, where the last surviving waters of the Zerafshan find their home in three small lakes, we reached the district so famous for its black, tightly curled lambskins, the Asiatic equivalent and superior to what in Europe we denominate Astrakhan. At the same time, curiously enough, the huge sheepskin bonnets, with which the Turkomans had rendered us familiar, disappeared in favour of the capacious white turban

In all the regions of the earth there is not a more flourishing or a more delightful country than the district of Bokhara.

of the Uzbeg or the Tajik. Early in the afternoon (we had left Amu Daria at 7 A.M.) there appeared over the trees on the north of the line a tall, graceful minaret, and the spherical outline of two large domes. We were in sight of Bokhara Es Sherif, or the Noble, at the present juncture the most interesting and intact city of the East. Skirting the city, from which we cannot at one moment have been more than four miles distant, and seeming to leave it behind, we stopped at the new Russian station of Bokhara, situated nearly ten miles from its gates.

Upon inquiry I found that the station had been very deliberately planted on this site. A committee, consisting of representatives of the Russian and Bokharan Governments and of merchants of both nationalities, had met to investigate and determine the question of locality. Some of the native merchants were in favour of a site nearer the town, though the general attitude of the Bokhariots towards the railway was then one of suspicion. It was regarded as foreign, subversive, anti-national, and even Satanic. Shaitan's Arba, or the Devil's Wagon, was what they called it. Accordingly, it was stipulated that the line should as far as possible avoid the cultivated land, and should pass at a distance of ten miles from the native city. This suggestion the Russians were not averse to adopting, as it supplied them with an excuse for building a rival Russian town around the station buildings, and for establishing a cantonment of troops to protect the latter, a step which might have been fraught with danger in

the nearer neighbourhood of the capital. Now, however, the Bokhariots are victims to much the same regrets as the wealthy English landowners who, when the railway was first introduced in this country, opposed at any cost its passage through their property. Already when the first working train steamed into Bokhara with rolling stock and material for the continuation of the line, the natives crowded down to see it, and half in fear, half in surprise, jumped into the empty wagons. Presently apprehension gave way to ecstasy. As soon as the line was in working order they would crowd into the open cars in hundreds, waiting for hours in sunshine, rain, or storm, for the engine to puff and the train to move. I found the third-class carriages reserved for Mussulman passengers crammed to suffocation, just as they are in India; the infantile mind of the Oriental deriving an endless delight from an excitement which he makes not the slightest effort to analyse or to solve. So great is the business now done at the station, that in September last General Annenkoff told a correspondent that since July the daily receipts from passenger and goods traffic combined had amounted to more than £300. Etiquette prevents the Amir himself from travelling by a method so repugnant to Oriental tradition; but he exhibits all the interest of reluctant ignorance, and seldom interviews a Russian without enquiring about its progress.

In a short time the new Russian town of which I have spoken will start into being. Plots of land adjoining the railway have been eagerly bought

The first working train steamed into Bokhara with rolling stock and material for the continuation of the line.

up by commercial companies, who will transfer their headquarters hither from the native city. An imposing station building had, when I visited it, risen to the height of two courses of stone above the ground. Barracks are to be built; streets will be laid out; a Residency will receive the Russian diplomatic Agent to the Amir, who now lives in the capital under limitations arising from his restricted surroundings, and from the fact that according to Bokharan etiquette every distinguished stranger in the city, himself included, becomes *ipso facto* a guest of the Amir, and is supplied with board and lodging. In another decade the new Bokhara will have attracted to itself much of the importance of the ancient city, and with its rise and growth the prestige of the latter must inevitably decline. Thus, by a seeming concession to native sentiment, the Russians are in reality playing their own game.

Before I describe my visit to the old Bokhara, I propose to append some observations upon the present political condition of the Khanate, a subject about which very scant and imperfect information appears ever to percolate to England.

The existing relations between Russia and Bokhara are defined by the two treaties of 1868 and 1873, both of which were concluded between Kaufmann, on behalf of the Imperial Government, and the late Amir Mozaffur-ed-din. These treaties left Bokhara, already shorn of Samarkand and the beautiful province of Zerafshan, in a position of qualified independence, the privileges of a court and native government being conceded in return for the surrender of the waterway of the Oxus, and of certain commanding fortified positions, to Russia. So closely, however, were the Russian toils cast round the Khanate that these conditions were generally recognised as involving ultimate absorption; and there was scarcely a single English writer who did not confidently predict that the death of the then Amir would infallibly be succeeded by total annexation. Sir Henry Rawlinson, by far the greatest English authority on Central Asia, expressed the following opinion (in an essay entitled "Later Phases of the Central Asian Question", written in December 1874): "As soon as there is rapid and direct communication between the Caucasus and Turkestan, a Russian Governor-General will take the place of the Amir, and then, if we may judge by our own Afghan experience, the Russian difficulties will commence." Mozaffur-ed-din has since died, and Turkestan is linked by a railway – the most rapid and direct of all communications – to the Caspian, and yet there is now, and is likely for some time to continue, an Amir of Bokhara. Russia has in fact played the part of sacrificing the shadow for the sake of the substance, and of tightening the iron grip beneath the velvet glove, with such adroitness and success that she can well afford for a time to leave the Khanate of Bokhara alone, with all the trouble and expense of annexation, and to tolerate a semi-independent Amir with as much complacency as we do a Khan of Khelat or a Maharajah of Kashmir. The analogy to Afghanistan is a faulty one, for the Bokhariots are not a turbulent or a fanatical people; and, though composed of several nationalities, present a fairly homogeneous whole.

The late Amir, who was a capable man, though a debauchee, died in 1885, leaving several sons. The complete ascendency of Russia was well illustrated by the events that ensued. Mozaffur had solicited the recognition as his heir of his fourth son, Seid Abdul Ahad, although the offspring of a slave; and this preference had been diplomatically humoured by the Russian Government, who sent the young man to St Petersburg (where now also they are educating his younger brother) and to Moscow, to imbibe Russian tastes and to be dazzled by the coronation of the Czar. In Eastern countries it is of the highest importance, immediately upon the occurrence of a vacancy to the throne, to have an official candidate forthcoming and to strike the first blow – a cardinal rule of action which Great Britain has uniformly neglected in her relations with Afghanistan. At the time of his father's death Abdul Ahad was Beg of Kermineh, a position which he held, even as a boy, during Schuyler's visit in 1873. The death of the old Amir was concealed for twelve hours; special messengers left at full gallop for Kermineh; the palace and troops were assured by the loyalty of the Kush-Begi or Grand Vizier, who marched out of the town to receive the new Amir. As soon as the death of Mozaffur leaked out the rumour was spread that a Russian general and army were advancing upon Bokhara; and when Abdul Ahad appeared, attended by General Annenkoff, whose presence in the vicinity had been judiciously turned to account, he entered into the inheritance of his fathers without difficulty and without striking a blow.

His eldest brother, Abdul Melik, who rebelled against his father eighteen years ago, has for some time been a fugitive in India, and is detained by the British Government at Abbotabad. Another elder brother, who was Beg of Hissar at the time of his brother's accession, and who also contemplated rebellion, was quietly removed as a State prisoner to Baisun. A third, who was similarly implicated, was deprived of his Begship of Tchiraktchi and incarcerated in the capital. The opposition, if it exists, has not dared to lift its head since.

Seid Abdul Ahad is a young man of twenty-eight or twenty-nine years of age, tall, black-bearded, and dignified in appearance. I saw him at Bokhara. Clad in magnificent robes, and riding at the head of a long cavalcade through the bazaar, he looked worthy to be an Oriental monarch. Little is publicly known of his character, which I heard variously described as inoffensive and avaricious. He is reputed among those who know him to be intelligent, and to understand the exact limits of his own independence. It is almost impossible to tell how far he is popular with his subjects, Oriental respect for the title outweighing all considerations of the personality of its bearer. Moreover, espionage is understood here, as elsewhere in the East, to play a prominent part in native *régimes*, and disloyalty is too dangerous to be common. If he can persuade his people that he is still something more than a gilded marionette, as the Russians are politic enough to allow him to do, and if at the same time he tacitly takes his orders from Tashkent, there is no reason why he should not retain his crown.

The Russians take great credit to themselves for having persuaded the

young sovereign to issue a decree, signed November 19, 1886, totally abolishing slavery in the State of Bokhara, and giving to each man a written certificate of his freedom – a step which would hardly have been necessary if Clause XVII of the Treaty of 1873 had been at all faithfully carried out.

The traffic in human beings, being contrary to the law which commands man to love his neighbour, is abolished for ever in the territory of the Khanate. In accordance with this resolve, the strictest injunctions shall be given by the Amir to all his Begs to enforce the new law, and special orders shall be sent to all border towns where slaves are transported for sale from neighbouring countries, that should any such slaves be brought there, they shall be taken from their owners and set at liberty without loss of time.

The relations between the two courts are in the capable hands of M. Tcharikoff, a most accomplished man, speaking English fluently – the result of an early Edinburgh education – and a thorough master of Oriental politics.

It was with no small astonishment that I found myself in the agreeable company of Dr. Heyfelder, approaching without let or hindrance the to Englishmen almost unknown city of Bokhara. I remembered having read in a notice in the *Westminster Review* of "Vambéry's Travels" the words written only thirteen years ago, "The very names of Khiva, Bokhara, and Samarkand are so associated with danger and difficulty that no European who is not prepared to take his life in his hand can venture to visit them." Even at Tiflis but a few weeks before, M. Henri Moser, the Swiss traveller, who six years ago visited Central Asia, and in 1886 published a most vivid and admirable account of his travels, entitled "A travers l'Asie Centrale," had warned me to be careful of the fanaticism of Bokhara, and had expressed a doubt as to whether a foreigner could obtain permission to enter the city. When he was there in 1883 himself, though in the company of a special envoy from the Czar, he remained a virtual prisoner indoors for three weeks, and was only once allowed to make an excursion through the town. I also remembered having read in the essay, already quoted, by Sir H. Rawlinson, "No one questions but that the general feeling at Bokhara is intensely hostile to Russia, and that the Amir has had and still has the utmost difficulty in preventing his subjects from breaking out and declaring a holy war against the infidels." And yet here was I, a stranger, and not even a Russian, approaching in absolute security this so-called haunt of bigotry, and about to spend several days in leisurely observation of its life and people.

Identified by some writers with the Bazaria of Quintus Curtius, where in the winter of B.C. 328, in the royal Chace or Paradise that had not been disturbed for four generations, Alexander the Great and his officers slew 4,000 animals, and where Alexander himself overcame a lion in single combat, extorting from the Spartan envoy the exclamation, "Well done, Alexander, nobly hast thou won the prize of kingship from the king of the

The Kush-Begi or Grand Vizier who marched out of the town to receive the new Amir.

woods!'' – generally derived from the Sanskrit name Vihara, or a college of wise men, associated in local legend with the mythical hero Afrasiab – there is little doubt that Bokhara is one of the most ancient cities in the East. Since it emerged into the light of history about 700 A.D., it has been alternately the spoil of the most famous conquerors and the capital of the greatest kings. Under the Iranian Samanid dynasty, who ruled for 130 years till 1000 A.D., it was regarded as a pillar of Islam and as the pride of Asia. Students flocked to its universities, where the most learned *mullahs* lectured; pilgrims crowded its shrines. A proverb said, "In all other parts of the world light descends upon earth, from holy Bokhara it ascends." Well-built canals carried streams of water through the city; luxuriant fruit-trees cast a shadow in its gardens; its silkworms spun the finest silk in Asia; its warehouses overflowed with carpets and brocades; the commerce of the East and West met and changed hands in its caravanserais; and the fluctuations of its market determined the exchange of the East. The Samanids were succeeded by the Turki Seljuks and the princes of Kharezm; and then, like a storm from the desert, there swept down upon Bokhara the pitiless fury of the Mongol, engulfing all in a like cataclysm of ruin. Jagatai and Oktai, sons of Jenghiz Khan, made some amends, by beneficent and merciful rule, for the atrocities of their father; and it was about this time that the elder brothers Polo, making their first voyage to the East, "si vindrent à une cité qui est appelée Bocara, moult noble et grant." A change of ownership occurred when about 1400 the great conqueror Timur – great, whether we regard him as savage, as soldier, or as statesman – overran the East, and established a Tartar dynasty that lasted a hundred years – a period which has been termed the Bokharan Renaissance. Another wave of conquest, the Uzbeg Tartars, ensued, again bringing to the surface two great names – that of Sheibani Mehemmed Khan, who overthrew the Timurid sovereigns and estabished an ethnical ascendency that has lasted ever since; and Abdullah Khan, the national hero of Bokhara, which owed to his liberal tastes much of its later architectural glory, its richly endowed colleges and its material prosperity. Subsequent dynasties, exhibiting a sorrowing record of incapacity, fanaticism, and decay, witnessed the gradual contraction of the once mighty empire of Transoxiana into a petty khanate. It is true that Bokhara still refers with pride to the rule of Amir Maasum, founder of the present or Manghit reigning family in 1784; but a bigoted devotee, wearing the dress and imitating the life of a dervish, was a poor substitute for the mighty sovereigns of the past. The dissolution of the times, yearly sinking into a deeper slough of vice, venality, and superstition, was fitly expressed in the character and reign of his grandson, the infamous Nasrullah (1826-1860), whose son, Mozaffur-ed-din (1860-1885), successively the foe, the ally, and the puppet of Russia, has left to his heir, the reigning Amir, a capital still breathing some aroma of its ancient glory, but a power whose wings have been ruthlessly clipped, and a kingdom indebted for a nominal independence to the calculating prudence rather than to the generosity of Russia.

English imagination has for centuries been stirred by the romantic associations of Bokhara, but English visitors have rarely penetrated to the spot. The first who reached its walls was the enterprising merchant Master Anthony Jenkinson, who was despatched on several adventurous expeditions to the East between 1557 and 1572, acting in the double capacity of ambassador to Queen Elizabeth and agent to the Muscovy Trading Company, which had been formed to open up the trade with the East. He stayed two and a half months in the city in the winter of 1558-59, being treated with much consideration by the sovereign, Abdullah Khan; and has left a record of his journey and residence in Bokhara, the facts of which display a minute correspondence (at which no one acquainted with the magnificent immobility of the East would express surprise) with the customs and manners of today. In the eighteenth century the record was limited to two names – Colonel Garber in 1732, and Mr. George Thompson in 1741. In this century William Moorcroft and George Trebeck, at the end of six years' wanderings from India, through Kashmir, Afghanistan, and Turkestan, reached Bokhara on February 25, 1825; leaving the city five months later only to die, the one at Andkui, the other at Mazar-i-Sherif. In 1832 Lieutenant, afterwards Sir Alexander Burnes, succeeded in reaching Bokhara also from India, in company with Dr. James Gerard, and in concluding a treaty of commerce with the Amir. Then in 1842 came the horrible tragedy which has inscribed the names of Stoddart and Conolly in the martyrology of English pioneers in the East. Sent in 1838 and 1840 upon a mission of diplomatic negotiation to the khanates of Central Asia, whose sympathies Great Britain desired to enlist in consequence of her advance into Afghanistan, they were thrown by the monster Nasrullah into a foul subterranean pit, infested with vermin, were subjected to abominable torture, and finally were publicly beheaded in 1842. Dr. Wolff, the missionary, travelling to Bokhara in 1843, in order to clear up their fate, ran many risks, but at length escaped with his life. For forty years, however, owing partly to the terror inspired by this disaster and to the perils of the journey, partly to the increasing influence of Russia, who did not encourage English intruders upon her new preserves, not a single Englishman set foot in Bokhara. A deep mystery overhung the place like a cloud, from which occasionally peeped the glint of Russian arms, or rang the voice of Russian cannon. A flash of light was thrown upon the prevailing darkness about halfway through this period by the heroic voyage of the Hungarian Vambéry, who penetrated to Bokhara in the garb of a mendicant dervish in 1863, and whose work, being published in English, awoke a profound sensation in this country. In 1873, Dr. Schuyler, the American, visited Bokhara under Russian patronage, in his tour through the Czar's dominions in Central Asia, and wrote a work which may be described as monumental, and is still a classic on the subject. Dr. Lansdell, the so-called missionary, was the next English visitor after Wolff, in 1882. I do not know of any others till the small batch who have obtained leave to go since the Transcaspian Railway was made, and whose experience it is my object to relate.

Upon our arrival at the station we committed ourselves to a *calèche* drawn by a *troika*, or team of three horses abreast, which had been sent down from the Russian Embassy in the city to meet us, and started for the capital. But for this good fortune we might have been compelled to make the journey either on donkey-back or in one of the huge wooden springless carts of the country called *arbas*, the wheels of which are from eight to ten feet high, and on whose elevated floor the natives squat contentedly, while the driver, usually seated on a saddle on the horse's back, urges the vehicle in the most casual manner over inequalities that would upset any less clumsy construction. Donkeys appeared to be the most popular method of locomotion, it being considered undignified in that country to walk. Two and even three men sit astride of the same diminutive animal, dangling their legs to the ground; or a bearded veteran, with his knees tilted up to his chin by the ridiculously short stirrups, would be seen perched upon a heap of saddle-bags, with a blue bale reared up behind him, which closer inspection revealed to be a daughter or a wife. Blinding clouds of dust, stirred by the great traffic, rolled along the road, which lay between orchards of mulberries, peaches, figs, and vines, or between fields in which the second grain crop of the year was already springing, or where hundreds of ripe melons littered the ground. We passed through several villages of low clay houses where dusty trees overhung the dry watercourses and thirsty camels stood about the wells, skirted a summer palace of the Amir surrounded by a mighty wall of sun-dried clay and at length saw drawn out in a long line before us the lofty ramparts of the city, with buttresses and towers, eight miles round, and pierced by eleven gates, open from sunrise to sunset, but hermetically closed at that hour against either exit or entrance till the morrow.

Entering by one of these, the Sallia Khaneh, we made our way for over two miles through a bewildering labyrinth of streets and alleys to the Russian Embassy, situated near the Ughlan Gate, at the far end of the city. This is a large native house with an extensive fruit garden surrounded by a clay wall, which was lent to the Russians by the Amir, who had confiscated it from its former owner, both for their own accommodation and for the entertainment of all distinguished guests. The servants, horses, grocery, and food are supplied by the Amir, one of whose officers, called the *Mirakhur* (literally Amir Akhor, *i.e.* Master of the Horse), lives in the outer court, and sits for the most part of the day smoking a pipe and tranquilly surveying operations. In one court are picketed the horses of the Russian guard, consisting of twenty Cossacks of the Ural. In the next are several guest-chambers, whose furniture consists of a carpet, a rope bedstead, and a table; and in a third are the offices and reception-rooms of the Embassy, all on a scale of similar unpretentiousness and in pure native style. On our table was spread every morning a *dastarkhan* (literally table-napkin) or collation of sugarplums, dried raisins, sweetmeats, and little cakes, together with a huge flat slab of brown bread – the traditional hospitality of the Amir. We never knew what to do with these dainties, which were not altogether to English taste, and the various plates with their contents became quite a

nuisance. Washing was rather a difficulty, because the only jug known to the natives is a brass ewer, which holds about as much as a teapot; and the only basin a receptacle with a small bowl in the middle of a large brim, the idea being that it is sufficient for water to be poured over the hands to ensure ablution. I created a great sensation with an indiarubber bath. Every morning the attendants brought in the provisions of the day for the entire household, consisting of mutton, chickens, and fruit; but the uncertain arrival and quantity of these rendered the hour of meals rather precarious. We were most hospitably welcomed by the Russian *attaché*, who, in the absence of M. Tcharikoff, the Resident, was acting as *chargé d' affaires*. He seemed to be overwhelmed with business, and deputations of the Amir's ministers, and other gorgeously robed officials were coming in and out the entire day. If we lost our way in the town, which it was almost impossible not to do, we had only to mention Eltchikhaneh, the name of the Embassy, to be at once shown the direction. I remember that as we reached our destination the sun was sinking. As its last rays lit up the horizon and threw the outline of dome and tower into picturesque relief, there rang through the cool calm air a chorus of piercing cries. The muezzins from a hundred minarets were calling the people to the Namaz, or evening prayer. In Bokhara, where the Mussulmans affect to be great purists, the Ezan, as it is called, is recited instead of chanted, the latter

The lofty ramparts of the city, with buttresses and towers, eight miles round, and pierced by eleven gates, open from sunrise to sunset, but hermetically closed at that hour.

151

being thought a heterodox corruption. For a minute or two the air is a Babel of sound. Then all sinks into silence and the shadows descend. At night the only sound is the melancholy beat of the watchman's drum as he patrols the streets with a lantern, no one being suffered abroad at that hour.

Bokhara is still a great city, for it numbers approximately one hundred thousand souls. Of these only one hundred and fifty are Europeans, nearly all of them Russians, Germans, or Poles. The bulk of the native population are Tajiks, the aboriginal Iranian stock, who may generally be distinguished from their Tartar brethren by the clearness and often by the brightness of their complexions, by the light colour of their hair and beards, sometimes a chestnut or reddish-brown, and by their more re-fined features. Tajik and Uzbeg alike are a handsome race, and a statelier urban population I never saw than in the streets and bazaars of the town. Every man grows a beard and wears an abundant white turban, consist-ing in the case of the orthodox of forty folds, and a long robe or *khalat* of striped cotton, or radiant silk, or parti-coloured cotton and silk. Bokhara has long set the fashion in Central Asia in the matter of dress, and is the great clothes mart of the East. Here the richness of Oriental fancy has expressed itself in the most daring but artistic combinations of colour. The brightest crimson and blue and purple and orange are juxtaposed or interlaced; and in Bokhara Joseph would have been looked upon as the recipient of no peculiar favour in the gift of a coat of many colours. Too

The Russian Embassy where washing was rather a difficulty.

often there is the most glaring contrast between the splendour of the exterior and the poverty that it covers. Many of the people are wretchedly poor; but living is absurdly cheap, and your pauper, undaunted by material woes, walks abroad with the dignity of a patriarch and in the garb of a prince.

Foreign elements are mingled in great numbers in the population. Slavery brought the Persians in old days to the Bokharan market, and has bequeathed to freedom their children and grandchildren. Usury brings the Hindus or Multani, as they are called, from a prevalent idea that Multan is the capital of India. With their dark complexions and lank black locks, with their tight dress and red caste marks on the forehead, they are an unmistakable lot. Living in caravanserais without wives or families they lead an unsocial existence and return to their country as soon as they have made their fortune. Neighbourhood brings the Kirghiz, the Turkomans, and the Afghans. Business brings to Bokhara, as it has taken all over the world, the Jews, who are here a singularly handsome people of mild feature and benign aspect. Confined to an Oriental *ghetto* and for long cruelly persecuted in Bokhara, they still exhibit in their prescribed dress and appearance the stamp of a peculiar people. The head is shaven save for two long locks hanging in a curl on either temple; they wear a square black calico bonnet trimmed with Astrakhan border, and a girdle round the wast. To my astonishment I met with one who could speak a little French.

One thing impressed itself very forcibly on my mind, namely, that Bokhara is not now a haunt of zealots, but a city of merchants. It contains a peaceful, industrious, artisan population utterly unfitted for war, and as wanting in martial instinct as in capacity. The hostility to strangers, and particularly to Christians, sometimes degenerating into the grossest fanaticism, upon which earlier travellers have enlarged, has either disappeared from closer contact with civilisation, or is prudently disguised. I attribute it rather to the former cause, and to the temperate conduct of the Russians in their dealings with the natives; because not even when I wandered about alone, and there was no motive for deception, did I observe the smallest indication of antagonism or repugnance. Many a face expressed that blank and haughty curiosity which the meanest Oriental can so easily assume; but I met with no rudeness or interference. On the contrary, the demeanour of the people was friendly, and no one when interrogated declined to answer a question. An acquaintance of the previous day would salute you as you passed by placing his hand on his breast and stroking his beard. I never quite knew what to do on these occasions. For not having a beard to stroke, I feared it might be thought undignified or contrary to etiquette to finger the empty air.

I have frequently been asked since my return – it is the question which an Englishman always seems to ask first – what the women of Bokhara were like? I am utterly unable to say. I never saw the features of one between the ages of ten and fifty. The little girls ran about, unveiled, in loose silk frocks, and wore their hair in long plaits escaping from a tiny skull-cap. Similarly the old hags were allowed to exhibit their innocuous

153

charms, on the ground, I suppose, that they could excite no dangerous emotions. But the bulk of the female population were veiled in a manner that defied and even repelled scrutiny. For not only were the features concealed behind a heavy black horsehair veil, falling from the top of the head to the bosom, but their figures were loosely wrapped up in big blue cotton dressing-gowns, the sleeves of which are not used but are pinned together over the shoulders at the back and hang down to the ground, where from under this shapeless mass of drapery appear a pair of feet encased in big leather boots. After this I should be more or less than human if I were to speak enthusiastically of the Bokharan ladies. Not even the generous though fanciful interpretation of Moore, who sang of

> that deep blue melancholy dress
> Bokhara's maidens wear in mindfulness
> Of friends or kindred, dead, or far away,

could reconcile me to so utter an abnegation of feminine duty.

From the people I pass to the city. In a place so arrogant of its spiritual reputation, it is not surprising that religious edifices should abound. Their number has, however, been greatly exaggerated. A devout Sunnite of Bokhara boasts that he can worship Allah in a different mosque on each day of the year. But this number must probably be halved. Similarly the alleged total of one hundred and sixty *medresses*, or religious colleges, is about double the actual figure. Both mosque and *medresse* are, with scarce an exception, in a state of great dilapidation and decay; the beautiful enamelled tiles, bearing in blue and white characters texts from the Koran, having fallen or been stripped from the lofty *pishtaks* or *façades*, and the interiors being in a state of great squalor. In a panorama of the city are conspicuous three domes covered with azure tiles. One of these belongs to the great mosque Musjid Baliand, or Kalian, variously reported to have been built or restored by Timur, where the Jumma, or Friday service, is held, attended by the Amir, and in the presence, theoretically, of the entire population. The mosque consists of a vast open court surrounded by a double and sometimes a triple colonnade. Here it was that in 1219 Jenghiz Khan, riding into the mosque, and, being told that it was the House of God, dismounted, ascended the pulpit, and flinging the Koran on to the ground, cried out: "The hay is cut; give your horses fodder" – a permission which his savage horde quickly interpreted as authority for a wholesale massacre. The two other domes surmount the largest *medresse* of Miri Arab, standing opposite, said to contain one hundred and fourteen cells, and to have attached to it two hundred and thirty *mullahs*, and exhibiting in its structural detail the best decorative work in Bokhara. These buildings are typical of the religious life and even of the faith of the people, which, in the degradation of morals so conspicuous in the East of this century, and partly owing to contact with a civilisation whose politic avoidance of proselytism or persecution has encouraged indifference, have become a hollow form, veiling hypocrisy and corruption. The fanaticism of the dervishes or *kalendars*, as they are

The Jews here are a singularly handsome people of mild feature and benign aspect.

155

Bokhara boasts the alleged total of one hundred and sixty medresses or religious colleges.

The Great Minaret whence criminals are thrown headlong.

called in the "Arabian Nights", of whom there used to be many orders in Bokhara, living in *tekkehs* or convents, and who stirred a dangerous bigotry by their wild movements and appeals, has subsided or taken the form of a mendicancy which, if unattractive, does not threaten a breach of the peace. Religious toleration, inculcated on the one side, has developed on the other with an astonishing rapidity.

Between the Musjid Baliand and the Miri Arab rises the tapering shaft of the Minari Kalian, or Great Minaret, whence criminals are thrown headlong, and which no European had hitherto been allowed to ascend. I have since heard that in the early part of the present year this rule was for the first time in history relaxed. The tower, which we had already seen from the railway, and which reminded me somewhat of the celebrated Kutub Minar, near Delhi, is nearly two hundred feet high, and is built of concentric rows of bricks stamped with decorative patterns, and converging towards the summit, there is an open gallery, on the roof of which reposes an enormous stork's nest. Some natives sitting at the base informed me that the keys were not forthcoming, but that on Fridays the doors flew mysteriously open. Their refusal to allow Christians to mount to the top has always been attributed to the fear that from that height sacrilegious eyes, looking down upon the flat roofs of the town, might

probe a little too deeply the secrets of female existence. I succeeded in obtaining a very fair panorama of the city by climbing to one of the highest points of the numerous cemeteries scattered throughout the place. From there was spread out around me a wilderness of flat clay roofs, above whose level surface towered the Ark or Citadel, built on a lofty mound, the Great Minaret, the ruined *pishtaks* of *medresses*, and the turquoise domes.

The Minari Kalian is still used for public execution, three criminals – a false coiner, a matricide, and a robber – having expiated their offences in this summary fashion during the last three years. Judgment is pronounced by the native tribunals, with whose jurisdiction the Russians have not made the smallest effort to interfere. The execution is fixed for a bazaar day, when the adjoining streets and the square at the base of the tower are crowded with people. The public crier proclaims aloud the guilt of the condemned man and the avenging justice of the sovereign. The culprit is then hurled from the summit, and, spinning through the air, is dashed to pieces on the hard ground at the base.

This mode of punishment, whose publicity and horror are well calculated to act as a deterrent among an Oriental population, is not the only surviving proof that the nineteenth century can scarcely be considered as yet to have got a firm hold upon Bokhara. But a short time before my visit the Divan Begi, second Minister of the Crown, eldest son of the Kush Begi, or Grand Vizier – the crafty old man who for many years has guided the policy of the Khanate, and whose memory extends back to the times of Stoddart and Conolly – was publicly assassinated by an Afghan in the streets. He was shot with two bullets, and soon after expired. Various explanations were given of this tragedy, one theory being that it was an act of private revenge for a recent official seizure of the murderer's property on account of taxes which he had refused to pay. Others contended that it was due to religious animosity, excited by the Persian descent and Shiite heresy of the slain man – his father, the Kush Begi, having been a Persian slave who rose to eminence by marrying a cast-off wife of the late Amir. But there seemed to be sufficient reason for believing that the act was really an expiring effort of outraged patriotism, the blow being directed against the minister who was supposed to be mainly responsible for the Russophile tendencies of the Government, and who had inflamed the indignation of the more bigoted of his countrymen by countenancing the advent of the railway, and thus setting the seal upon Bokharan humiliation. Whichever of these explanations be correct, the murderer was successful in his object, but paid the penalty by a fate consecrated in the immemorial traditions of Bokhara, though a startling incident under the new *régime*.

He was handed over by the Amir to the relatives of the murdered man that they might do with him what they willed. By them he was beaten with sticks and stabbed with knives. Accounts vary as to the actual amount of torture inflicted upon the miserable wretch; but it is said that his eyelids were cut off or his eyes gouged out. In this agonising condition he was tied to the tail of an ass and dragged through the streets of the town

to the market-place, where his body was quartered and thrown to the dogs. It is consoling to know that this brutal atrocity – the *vendetta* of the East, the old savage law of an eye for an eye and a tooth for a tooth – was enacted in the absence of the Russian Resident, who, it is to be hoped, would have interfered to prevent its accomplishment had he been upon the spot.

The interior of the city is a wilderness of crooked alleys, winding irregularly between the blind walls of clay-built houses, which are without windows and have no aperture in their front but closely barred wooden doors. Trees line one of the principal streets and hang above the frequent tanks and pools, which are neither so large, so well filled, or so clean as those in Indian towns. On the contrary, the water is often low and stagnant; and if the pool is in the neighbourhood of a mosque, being considered holy, it is used for drinking as well as for washing purposes, and spreads the germs of the various endemic diseases. The largest of these reservoirs is the Liabehaus Divan Begi, near one of the most frequented mosques. Eight rows of stone steps descend to the water, in which men are always dipping their hands. The surrounding space is a popular lounge; and cooked meats, confectionery, fruits, and tea are dispensed from rows of stalls under an avenue of mulberry-trees.

The interior of the city is a wilderness of crooked alleys.

From dawn to sunset the largest crowd is collected in the Righistan or market-place in the north-west of the town. Every square foot of the surface is occupied by stalls and booths, which are frequently shaded by awnings of woven reed balanced on poles like the umbrellas of the *fakirs* on the banks of the Ganges at Benares. Here men come to buy provisions, meat, flowers, and fruit. The butchers' counters are covered with the *kundiuks* or fat rumps of the so-called big-tailed sheep, of which Marco Polo said, six hundred years ago, that "they weigh thirty pounds and upwards, and are fat and excellent to eat." Blocks of rose-coloured rock salt from the mines near Karshi were exposed in great abundance. Flowers appeared to be very popular, and many of the men wore a sprig of yellow blossom stuck behind the ear. Street vendors of meat went about shouting their wares, which consisted of kebabs and patties on trays. Fruit was extraordinarily luxuriant and good. Magnificent melons were sold at not more than a farthing apiece; and the price of luscious white grapes was only a rouble (two shillings) for eight pouds, or 288 English lbs. Peaches, apricots, and the celebrated Bokharan plums were not then in season. Not far away was the horse and donkey market; a horse might be bought for any price from 5s. to £30; but a very respectable animal would cost about £10.

At the extremity of the Righistan rises the Ark or Citadel, originally built by Alp Arslan, over 800 years ago, upon a lofty natural elevation a mile in circumference, and surrounded by a high battlemented wall. The entrance gateway, erected by Nadir Shah in 1742, is approached by a paved slope and leads between two towers, above which is fixed the European clock made for the tyrant Nasrullah by the Italian prisoner, Giovanni Orlandi, as the ransom for his life. Within the Ark are situated the palaces of the Amir and the Kush Begi, the Treasury, the public offices, three mosques, and the State prison. Sauntering out one morning quite early I endeavoured to penetrate into its interior, but was stopped and sent back by the frowns and gesticulations of a crowd of natives seated in the doorway. Somewhere in this pile of buildings was the horrible hole, or bug-pit, into which Stoddart and Conolly were thrown. It is said for some time to have been sealed up, though the fact that quite recently this was a common mode of Bokharan punishment is proved by the experience of the French travellers MM. Bonvalot and Capus, who visited the Bokharan fortress of Karshi in 1882, and were shown there a subterranean hole from which a sickening stench exhaled, and in which they heard the clank of chains, and saw the uplifted despairing hands of the poor wretches immured below. The *Times* correspondent who visited Bokhara a few months before I did was shown a part of the existing Zindan or prison, which he described in a letter to the *Times* (October 2, 1888). But either the officials must have had intimation of his visit, or he was not shown the worst part; for one of my companions, being admitted without warning, found one hundred prisoners huddled together in a low room, and chained to each other by iron collars round their necks, wooden manacles on their hands, and fetters on their feet, so that they could neither stand nor turn nor scarcely move. The Zindan,

The Palace of the Amir.

however, is not the same as the Kana Khaneh, where Stoddart was tortured; nor must the dungeon, now covered up with a slab in the floor of the former, which the *Times* correspondent was shown, be confused with the famous bug-pit. The Zindan with its two compartments, the upper and lower (*i.e.* subterranean) dungeons, were and are outside the Ark. The Kana Khaneh was inside it, near the entrance from the Righistan. M. Tcharikoff, the Resident, told me at Tashkent that the present Amir upon his accession shut up one of these prisons, the hundred and thirteen criminals who had long lain there being brought out, some of them beaten, and a few executed, but the majority released; and it may have been to the Ab Khaneh, with its *annexe* the Kana Khaneh, that he referred. However this be, the facts I have related will show that there still remains much to be done in mitigating the barbarity of native rule.

At all hours the most interesting portion of the city is the Tcharsu, or Great Bazaar, one of the largest and most important in the East. It covers a vast extent of ground, and is said to consist of thirty or forty separate bazaars, of twenty-four caravanserais for the storage of goods and accommodation of merchants, and of six *timis*, or circular vaulted spaces, from which radiate the principal alleys, shaded with mats from the sun, and crowded with human beings on donkey-back, on horseback, and on foot. Huge *arbas* crash through the narrow streets and just shave

The Great Bazaar, one of the largest and most important in the East.

the counters on either hand. Behind these, in small cupboard-like shops, squat the Oriental tradesmen surrounded by their wares. Long lines of splendid camels laden with bales of cotton march superciliously along, attached to each other by a rope bound round the nose, the cartilage of which is forbidden to be pierced, in the familiar fashion of the East, by a humane decree of the late Amir.

In different parts we may see the armourers' shops, the turners' shops, where the workman turns a primitive lathe by the aid of a bowstring; the vendors of brightly painted red and green wooden saddles with tremendous pommels inlaid with ivory; of *shabraques*, or saddlecloths, a speciality of Bokhara, made of crimson velvet gorgeously embroidered with gold and silver thread, and powdered with silver spangles; of black, curly lambskin fleeces from Kara Kul; of leather belts stuck with knives; of the bright green tobacco or snuff which the natives chew with great avidity, and which is carried in a tiny gourd fastened with a stopper; of pottery, coarse in texture but spirited in design; of water-pipes, or *tchilim*, in which two tubes project from a brass-mounted gourd, one of them holding the charcoal and tobacco, the other for the smoker's mouth; of embroideries executed in large flowery patterns, and for the most part in crimson silk on a cotton ground, by a needle fixed in a wooden handle like a gimlet. Elsewhere are the bazaars for harness, carpets, rope, iron, hardware, skins, dried fruits, and drugs, the latter containing, in addition to medicines, cosmetics for the ladies' eyebrows and lashes, and rouge for their cheeks and nails. Whole streets are devoted to the sale of cotton goods, gaudy Bokharan velvets and rainbow-coloured native silks and tissues. Here leather riding-trousers, or *chumbar*, are procurable, stained red with madder, and showily embroidered with silk down the front. There are displayed green leather boots all in one piece, or long riding-boots with turned-up toes and ridiculously sharp-pointed heels.

Russian *samovars*, or tea-urns, are sold in great numbers, and one simmers in almost every shop, tea being as constant a beverage here as it is in Japan, or as coffee is in Constantinople. I thought the jewellery insignificant and poor. But, on the other hand, the brass and copper work, which is confined to a separate bazaar, resounding the whole day with a mighty din of hammers, is original and beautiful. Elegant *kungans*, or brass ewers, may be purchased; and every variety of bowl, beaten into quaint designs and shapes, or with a pattern chiselled into the metal through a surface coating of tin. I was more than once offered silver coins of the Graeco-Bactrian dynasty, bearing the inscription $BA\Sigma I\Lambda EY\Sigma\ EY\Theta Y\Delta HMO\Sigma$.

Bargaining was only to be pursued with great patience and much cajolery, the vendor being as a rule by no means anxious to part with his article except for a considerable profit. Crowds will collect round a European as he is endeavouring to make a purchase, following each stage of the transaction with the keenest interest, and applauding the rival strategy. The object under discussion will be passed from hand to hand, and each will give his own opinion. Usually a volunteer middleman detaches himself from the crowd, and with a great show of disinterestedness affects to conciliate the owner and to complete the bargain. A good deal of gesticulation must of necessity be employed, for with a total ignorance of Tartar on the one side, and of English, German, or French on the other, and only an infinitesimal command of Russian on both, progress is difficult. The shopkeeper is very amenable to personal attention. He likes to be patted on the back and whispered to in the ear; and if, after a prolonged struggle, repeated perhaps for two or three days, you can at length get hold of his hand and give it a hearty shake, the bargain is clinched and the purchase is yours. The people struck me as very stupid in their computations, requiring calculating-frames with rows of beads in order to make the simplest reckoning, and being very slow in exchange. But I thought them a far less extortionate and rascally lot than their fellows in the marts of Cairo or Stamboul. Jenkinson's description of the Bokharan currency still holds good:

Their money is silver and copper; for golde, there is none currant; they have but one piece of silver, and that is worth 12 pence English; and the copper money are called pooles, and 120 of them goeth to the value of the said 12d., and is more common paiment than the silver.

At the time of my visit the silver *tenga* was worth about fivepence, and contained sixty-five of the little copper *puls*.

It is quite evident that the Russians possess a complete monopoly of the important trade from Europe. Earlier travellers report having seen many Birmingham and Manchester goods. I only noticed one shop where English wares were being sold, and they had come through a Bombay firm. Russian prints, calicoes, and cottons are successfully competing with the far more beautiful native materials, and hideous brocades from Moscow debauch the instinctive good taste of the East. Russian iron, hardware, and porcelain have driven out the native manufacture of these articles. European ink, pens, writing-paper, and note-books are exposed for sale. Kerosene lamps are beginning to take the place of the mutton-grease candles, till a year ago the only means of lighting, and the sewing-machine buzzes in the cotton-seller's shop. Since my return I have heard that the entire town is about to be lighted with petroleum.

At all the railway stations along the line is to be found a plentiful display of liquor and spirits, in the fantastic glass bottles, shaped like animals, that the Russian taste affects. The Russian soldier in Central Asia has an excuse for insobriety in the loneliness of his life and the want of more elevating pastime. But his example is unhappily contagious. The Mussulmans of the Caucasus have long ago waived their scruples; the Persians of Khorasan have been similarly seduced by Russian importation, and it is to be expected that artificial restrictions will not save the more orthodox Sunnites of Bokhara from a like surrender. Already the Khans of Merv, habituated to European entertainment, sip their glass of vodka, and toss off their bumper of champagne. Where costliness does not intervene, the licence of an upper class is soon apt to become the law of a lower. Western civilisation in its Eastward march suggests no sadder reflection than that it cannot convey its virtues alone, but must come with Harpies in its train, and smirch with their foul contact the immemorial simplicity of Oriental life.

Nevertheless in many respects the latter still remains intact. Customs and methods prevail which date from an unknown antiquity, and alternately transport the observer to the Bagdad of Haroun al Raschid and to the Hebrews of the Mosaic dispensation. In a low dark hovel I saw corn being ground by a miserable horse who, with blinded eyes and his nose tied to a beam overhead, was walking round and round a narrow circle, and causing to revolve an upper and a nether millstone below the surface of the ground. I saw cotton being carded by the primitive agency of a double bow, the smaller one being fixed to the ceiling and the larger one attached to its string by a cord, and struck by a mallet so as to cause a smart rebound. One morning in the bazaar we observed a crowd collected in the street round a mounted horseman, and presently howls of pain issued from the centre of the throng. It turned out to be the Reis-i-shariat, a religious functionary or censor of morals – an office which was revived a century ago by Amir Maasum – whose duty it is to ride about the town, compelling people to attend the schools or mosques, and inspecting weights and measures. He was engaged upon the latter operation, and was comparing the stone weights in a shop, which are often substituted for metal because of their cheapness, with the standard weight. The luckless shopkeeper, convicted of fraud, was forthwith stripped bare in the street, forced to kneel down, and soundly castigated on the back with a leather thong whip, carried by the Reis' attendants. The features of the crowd expressed a faint curiosity, but not a trace of another emotion.

It would be hard to exaggerate the part which the manners and generosity of Dr. Heyfelder, who has now lived for nearly two years in Bokhara, have played in the pacification of this whilom haunt of fanaticism. As early as six in the morning people crowd into the Embassy to see him. Very often so childish is their faith that they do not ask for a prescription, but simply implore his touch. At first the women declined to unveil, would not allow him to feel their pulse, and only communicated with him through the medium of a male relative. Familiarity, however, is fast obliterating this suspicion. When the lately murdered Divan Begi was lying on his deathbed, and his life blood was ebbing away, he kept asking every few minutes for his doctor. The latter was unfortunately at a distance, and, owing to a block on the railway, could not come. A fat old Beg, he told me, came to him one day and said, "Can you make me better? I suffer from eating four dinners a day." "Certainly," said the doctor, "eat three." Thereupon the old gentleman became very angry, and retorted, "How can I eat less when I am called upon to entertain venerable guests?" When the young Amir came back from the coronation of the Czar in Russia, Dr. Heyfelder asked him what he had liked best in that country. "The lemonade and ice at Moscow," was the ingenuous reply; an answer which reminds one of O'Donovan's tale of the man who had been a servant of the Persian Embassy in London for nine years, and who, having returned to his native land, said that his dearest recollections of the British metropolis were its corned beef and bitter ale.

The object in which the doctor is specially interested is the extirpation of the well-known Bokharan disease, the *reshta*, or *filaria medinensis*, a parasite which cannot even now be better described than in the words of Anthony Jenkinson three hundred years ago:

There is a little river running through the middes of the saide Citie, but the water thereof is most unwholsome, for it breedeth sometimes in men that drinke thereof, and especially in them that be not there borne, a worme of an ell long, which lieth commonly in the legge betwixt the flesh and the skinne, and is pluckt out about the ancle with great art and cunning; the Surgeons being much practised therein, and if shee breake in plucking out, the partie dieth, and every day she commeth out about an inche, which is rolled up, and so worketh till shee be all out.

So common is this malady in Bokhara, that every fifth person suffers from it; and the same individual may be harbouring at the same time from two to ten, nay, from twenty to thirty, of these worms. Khanikoff even relates that he heard of a Khivan who had one hundred and twenty simultaneously in his body. Their extraction is not difficult or dangerous, unless, as Jenkinson said, part of the worm is broken off and left in the flesh, when suppuration and consequent risk may ensue. When extracted it is sometimes from two to three feet long, and has the appearance of a long string of vermicelli. A curious feature is, that the most minute examination of the drinking-water of Bokhara under the microscope has never revealed the *reshta* germ. Nor, again, has Dr. Heyfelder ever discovered or identified a male specimen. He is inclined to think that the female, being oviparous, pushes her way to the surface of the skin when full of young – each reshta, upon dissection, being found to contain from half a million to a million embryo worms. Either the male dies after fertilisation, or the parasite is bisexual. The embryos, if occasionally dosed with a drop of water, will continue to live for six days. The doctor has made frequent efforts to obtain statistics from the natives both at Bokhara and Samarkand, as to the character, area, and probable causes of the affliction, but has failed to obtain any replies. It is by no means certain even that it is necessarily to be traced to the waters of the Zerafshan. Higher up the river it is more rare. At Kermineh it is quite an exception, at Samarkand it is only found when imported, and at Jizak, once a centre of the disease, it has been immensely reduced since the Russian occupation and superintendence of the water supply. The filthy condition of some of the open pools at Bokhara is quite sufficient to account for its wide propagation in that place. One of the commonest causes of reproduction is the shocking carelessness of the barbers, who are the professional extractors of the worm, and who throw down the living parasite, which very likely crawls away and multiplies its species a hundred-thousand-fold in some pool or puddle. Dr. Heyfelder would have a law passed that every reshta shall be burned upon extraction. The disease could, however, only be eradicated by a very stringent supervision of the water supply, and by the compulsory use of filters; the latter being the means by which the Russians, while constructing the railway, entirely escaped contagion.

Among the prerogatives which are left to the Amir are the possession of a native army, and the insignia and retinue of an Asiatic Court. The former is said to consist of about 12,000 men (in Vambéry's time it was 40,000), but resembles an irregular gendarmerie rather than a standing army. I expect that its value, which might be guessed by analogy with the least warlike forces of the native princes in India, was very accurately gauged by General Komaroff, who smiled when I asked him if he thought the Bokharan soldiers were any good, and said, "They are possibly better than the Persians." It is quite laughable to hear, as we have recently done, of their being moved down to the Oxus to resist the Afghans. Their uniform consists of a black sheepskin shako, a loose red tunic with leather belt and cartridge-pouch, abundant pantaloons, and big leather boots. It is closely modelled on the Russian lines, and includes even Russian shoulder-straps. Each soldier is armed with some kind of musket and a sword; and the words of command, which were framed by a Cossack deserter named Popoff, who organised the army for the late Amir, are delivered in a mixture of Russian, Tartar, and English. The men are said to be volunteers, and while serving to receive pay equal to from £10 to £20 a year. There are also reported to be two squadrons of cavalry and ten pieces of artillery. The ideal of military efficiency in Bokhara seems to be limited to precision in drill, in which I was assured by some European officers that they are very successful. Every movement is smartly executed to the sound of a bugle, and the voice of the officers, whose uniform is fantastic and appearance contemptible, is never heard. There are some 150 signals, which it is not surprising to hear that it takes a man several years to learn. Where the British soldier is ordered to pile arms and to stand at ease, the Bokharan sits down on the ground. Some years ago the drill contained a movement of a most interesting character which has since been abandoned. At a given signal the soldiers lay down upon their backs, and kicked their heels in the air. This was copied from the action of Russian troops in one of the earlier engagements, where, after crossing a river, they were ordered to lie down and shake the water out of their big top-boots. The retreating Bokhariots saw the manoeuvre, and attributed to it a magical share in the Russian victory.

Military efficiency in Bokhara seems to be limited to precision in drill.

The Bokharan Court is still surrounded by all the pomp and much of the mystery of an Asiatic *régime*. The Amir is treated as a sort of demigod, whom inferior beings may admire from a distance. No glimpse is ever caught of the royal harem. *Batchas*, or dancing boys, are among the inseparable accessories of the palace, and represent a Bokharan taste as effeminate as it is depraved. An audience with the Amir is attended with much formality, and is followed on his part by an offering of gifts. No European can be presented except in uniform or in evening dress. One of my companions, who was a relative of the Governor-General, having been granted an audience, found that he had not the requisite garments in which to go. Accordingly I had to rig him out in my evening clothes with a white tie and a Bond Street shirt. Etiquette further requires the presentee to ride to the palace on horseback; and a more comic spectacle than an English gentleman in a dress-suit riding in broad daylight in the middle of a gaudily dressed cavalcade through an Oriental town cannot be conceived. At such moments even the English breast yearns for a decoration. When the audience is over a dastarkhan is served, one or more horse with embroidered saddlecloths and turquoise-studded bridles are brought in, and he "whom the king delighteth to honour" is sent home with a wardrobe full of brilliant *khalats*.

The narrative of my experiences at Bokhara will no doubt leave the same impression upon the minds of my readers as did their occurrence upon my own, viz. one of astonishment at the extraordinary change which must have been effected in the attitude and demeanour of the people during the last few years. If the accounts that were received up to that date about the hostility of the inhabitants be true, it amounts to little less than a political revolution. Whether this be due to a merely interested recognition of the overwhelming strength of Russia, or to the skilful diplomacy of the latter, or, as General Komaroff hinted to me, to the salutary and all-powerful influence of the rouble, it must equally be set down to the credit of the conquering power. The allegiance of the Amir may be considered as absolutely assured; not only because a treacherous move would at once cost him his throne, but because Russia, having possession of the upper courses of the Zerafshan, could cut off the water supply of Bokhara in a week, and starve the city into submission.

What diplomacy began the railway is fast completing. So mercantile, and, it may be added, so mercenary a people as the Bokhariots, fall ready victims to the friendly stress of commercial fusion. Native finance is itself an indirect ally of Russia; for gradually, as trade is developed, the 2½ per cent *ad valorem* duty, both upon exports and imports, which is still levied under the terms of the Treaty of 1873, as well as the heavy local taxation, amounting to nearly 1s. 6d. in the pound, exclusive of the tithe to the Mosque, which is exacted from the subjects of the Amir, as compared with those of the Czar, will operate as inducements towards a closer union.

Looking forward into the future, I anticipate that Bokhara may still for many years remain a *quasi* independent State, but that the capital will gradually succumb to Russian influence and civilisation, and that so in time a party may arise among the natives themselves agitating for incorporation.

For my own part, on leaving the city I could not help rejoicing at having seen it in what may be described as the twilight epoch of its glory. Were I to go again in later years it might be to find electric light in the highways. The King of Korea has it at Seoul, a surely inferior capital; the Amir of Afghanistan has it at Kabul; then why not he of Bokhara? It might be to see window-panes in the houses, and to meet with trousered figures in the streets. It might be to eat *zakuska* in a Russian restaurant and to sleep in a Russian hotel; to be ushered by a *tchinovnik* into the palace of the Ark, and to climb for fifty *kopecks* the Minari Kalian. Who can tell whether Russian beer will not have supplanted tea, and *vodka* have supplemented opium? Civilisation may ride in the Devil's Wagon, but the devil has a habit of exacting his toll. What could be said for a Bokhara without a Kush Begi, a Divan Begi, and an Inak – without its *mullahs* and *kalendars*, its *toksabas* and its *mirzabashi*, its *shabraques* and *tchapans* and *khalats*? Already the mist of ages is beginning to rise and to dissolve. The lineaments are losing their beautiful vague mystery of outline. It is something, in the short interval between the old order and the new, to have seen Bokhara, while it may still be called the Noble, and before it has ceased to be the most interesting city in the world.

Samarkand and Tashkent

Towns also and cities, especially the ancient, I failed not to look upon with interest. How beautiful to see thereby, as through a long vista, into the remote Time; to have, as it were, an actual section of almost the earliest Past brought safe into the Present, and set before your eyes!
CARLYLE, *Sartor Resartus*.

BOKHARA is about 150 miles by rail from Samarkand, and the only two important points *en route* are the Bokharan fortress of Kermineh, which the railway skirts at a distance of five miles, and the Russian frontier post of Katta Kurgan, where we enter the Zerafshan province, annexed by Russia in 1868, after the war with Bokhara that resulted in the capture of Samarkand. A very wise step this was; for the basin of the Zerafshan river, or Gold Strewer, the Polytimetus, or Very Precious, of the Greeks, which extends for about 250 miles between parallel ranges of mountains, is a veritable garden of Eden, and incomparably the most fertile part of Central Asia. The country is laid out less frequently in fields than in orchards, producing grapes, figs, peaches, mulberries, apricots, almonds, plums, pomegranates, apples, and pears, and giving a return seven times more profitable than that from agriculture. Branches of the Zerafshan, or canals dug from the main stream, form a network over the face of the land, upon which the eye traces their course in lines of osier and willow, separating brilliant *parterres* of green. The wealth of this natural El Dorado is entirely water-derived and water-fed, and depends upon a system of canalisation that is described by Arab historians as having prevailed unchanged in the ninth century A.D., the origin of which is fixed by many before the Christian era, and which by some has even been thought to vie in antiquity with the kindred system in Egypt.

I do not propose here to give a detailed account of the Bokharan irrigation works, because this is a subject that has already fully, and perhaps more properly, been dealt with in other works. Its most curious feature to the eyes of a stranger is the extent to which, in spite of Russian influence and a twenty years' possession, native tradition and methods are still pursued. The Russians made some effort at first to remodel the entire system on more modern and scientific lines; and a Russian official, assisted by native experts, is still responsible for the province of Samarkand. On the whole, however, it has been found best to leave alone both the existing machinery, which depends in the last resort upon popular election by the cultivators of the soil, and the immemorial methods, which, though devised without scientific appliances or knowledge of hydraulics, have yet been conceived with extreme ingenuity and are passably adapted to fulfil their purpose. In Bokhara this system leads to a good deal of abuse; for the *Mirab*, or "Lord of the waters", who is appointed to administer the water supply of a particular district, is neither an engineer nor an expert, but commonly a Court

169

nominee, who owes his selection to favouritism, and, like a Roman Verres, does his best to convert his tenure of office into a policy of insurance against future contingencies. Nevertheless it is said that the people most interested, viz. the cultivators of the soil, are satisfied, and that any attempt to enforce a different, even if a more technical, system would lead to mutiny.

In the territory of Bokhara the extent of the irrigation works may be estimated from the fact that the Zerafshan river has forty-three principal canals diverted from the parent stream, with a total length of not less than 600 miles, in addition to eighty-three similar main canals in the Samarkand province, as well as 939 branch canals conducted from them. The breadth of the canals varies from six to sixty feet. They are not straight, but sinuous and meandering, often forming ravines and gullies, and generally occupying far more space than is absolutely necessary to conduct water. Any inequality of distribution is speedily rectified upon the frantic complaints of the suffering or imperilled districts; and the more fortunate or better provided have their supplies temporarily arrested or curtailed for the relief of their destitute brethren. It is said, notwithstanding, that Bokhara, being lower down the stream than Samarkand, is the loser in any partition, however fairly carried out, and that owing to the steadily diminishing supply from the uplands, the oasis is being contracted, and is yearly ceding some of its fringes to the implacable encroachment of the dunes. Certain it is, that cities and oases within twenty miles of the capital have been so overtaken and destroyed, and that the sand-flood is advancing rather than retreating. There are some who see in this movement a sentence of impending doom against Bokhara, and proclaim that the handwriting is already upon the wall. If those who live upon the spot take a less pessimistic view, it may be because they know that its realisation will not occur in their time, or that they have confidence, both in the schemes of forestry and water-storage which the Russians have to some extent taken in hand, and in the last emergency in the resources of science, to save them from so grim a consummation.

Greater unity as well as competence of administration are reforms, apart from more economical and scientific methods, which it is well within the power of Russia to introduce. A more equable system of land taxation would follow next upon the programme; and from neither need any result, other than favourable, be anticipated, while regard could be had in both cases to the prejudices and prescriptions of the natives.

The Samarkand district, which we now enter, contains, according to the latest statistics, upon an area of 24,184 square versts, a population of 464,985 inhabitants, of whom 452,844 are natives, 9,397 Russians, 2,653 Jews, 81 Hindus, and 10 non-Russian Europeans. The bulk of the people, not congregated in the big towns, are engaged in agriculture or horticulture. We may infer the marvellous fertility of the soil and the alluvial bounty of the Zerafshan from the fact that three crops are sometimes raised from the same plot in one year: (1) the winter crop of wheat, barley, rye, or clover, sown in November and reaped in the early spring; (2) the spring crop of maize, rice, sorghum, or cotton, sown in the spring and reaped in the early autumn; and (3) the autumn crop of turnips, carrots, or millet, sown in September or October and gathered in November. Clover can be cut five or six times in the year. Through scenery and amid surroundings of which these statistics may have furnished, not a picture but an adumbration, the traveller approaches the most famous and romantic city in Central Asia, Samarkand.

Of the history of Samarkand – the Maracanda of the Macedonians, the Samokien of the Buddhist pilgrim Hiouen Tsang, the Sumar Margo of Sir John Mandeville, the favourite and also the final resting-place of Timur, the capital, with 150,000 inhabitants, of Sultan Baber, the combined Athens and Delphi of the remote East – I shall here say nothing. Whatever historical allusions have been justified in treating of other and less widely known places, are superfluous in the mention of a spot that has long been dear not only to the informed zeal of the student, but to the cultured intelligence of the world.

Neither shall I feel justified in giving more than a cursory account of the great monuments that once made Samarkand the glory, and that still, in their ruin, leave it the wonder, of the Asiatic continent. They have in the main been so well and conscientiously described in Schuyler's and other writings, and, beyond the march of further decay, have altered so little since their date, that were I to linger over details I might be convicted of recapitulating badly what had been excellently said before. The illustrations which are appended will give my readers some idea of their present condition; while such remarks as I shall venture to make upon them will be the independent suggestions of the writer's observation. The very purport of this book, already, I fear, somewhat strained in the chapter upon the city of Bokhara, compels me to turn aside, with whatever reluctance, from the splendours of the ancient to the more modest but still appreciable attractions of the modern town.

The present terminus of the railway at Samarkand is a scene of great activity; for the station buildings and offices were, when I visited them, still in the hands of the masons and had not yet reached the first storey. A broad but dusty road, the first metalled road I had seen east of the Caspian, planted on both sides with avenues of poplars, runs for a distance of nearly three miles to the Russian town. This is a delightful quarter, completely buried in trees, from which peep out the white fronts of low one-storeyed houses, and is intersected at right angles by boulevards of enormous width overshadowed by lines of poplars and acacias, and bordered by rivulets of running water. The principal street is planted with as many as twelve parallel rows of trees, on either side of the carriage drive, the footpaths, and the brawling streams. From an elevation no buildings are visible, and the Russian town might be mistaken for a thickly wooded park. From the earliest times this side of Samarkand has been celebrated for its wealth of trees and verdure, and for its sylvan retreats, the favourite residence in bygone days of Tartar nobles, just as they now are of Russian generals and colonels. In the tenth century Ibn Haukal left on record that

There are here many villas and orchards, and very few of the palaces are without gardens, so that if a person should go to the Kohendiz, and from that look around, he would find that the villas and palaces were covered, as it were, with trees; and even the streets and shops and banks of the streams are all planted with trees.

And in 1404, Don Ruy de Clavijo, visiting Samarkand when at the height of its glory under Timur, wrote this interesting though perhaps insufficiently concise description:

The city is surrounded on all sides by many gardens and vineyards, which extend in some directions a league and a half, in others two leagues, the city being in the middle. Among these gardens there are great and noble houses, and here the lord (*i.e.* Timur) has several palaces. The nobles of the city have their houses amongst these gardens, and they are so extensive, that when a man approaches the city he sees nothing but a mass of very high trees. Many streams of water flow through the city and through these gardens, and among these gardens there are many cotton-plantations and melon-grounds, and the melons of this ground are good and plentiful; and at Christmas-time there is a wonderful quantity of melons and grapes.

Embowered here and there amid these agreeable surroundings are to be seen modern buildings of some pretentiousness and importance. Of these the largest is the Governor's house.

Embowered here and there amid these agreeable surroundings are to be seen modern buildings of some pretentiousness and importance. Of these the largest are the Governor's house, standing in a fine park; the military club, similarly situated, and the Russian church with blue star-bespangled domes. There are also some public gardens containing a lake. A certain primness and monotony of appearance may perhaps be charged against the Russian Samarkand. But compared with other places I had seen it was almost a paradise; and if life there be regarded as exile, at least it can be no insupportable burden. The climate is delicious, the elevation above the sea is considerable -- over 2,000 feet – and there is a civilised society.

Here, however, as elsewhere, the railway is effecting a most extraordinary change. Tolerable though existence may have been at Samarkand under the old conditions, it was yet very remote, more remote than Tashkent, through which place it was commonly approached from the north. The post took nearly a month in arriving from St. Petersburg. A telegram to Bokhara, only 150 miles distant, was obliged to describe a circuit of many thousands of miles by Tashkent, Orenburg, Samara, Moscow, and Baku, and very likely did not reach its destination for days. A far-off echo of the great world dimly permeated months afterwards to the banks of the Zerafshan, like the faint murmur in the hollow of a sea-shell. General Annenkoff's railway has changed all this. It has completed the work which a twenty years' occupation had previously set in train. Already the old times, when a Bokharan Amir took his seat upon the *Koktash*, and when a desperate attempt was made to entrap and massacre the Russian garrison in the citadel, have lapsed from memory;

and the present generation of Uzbeg and Tajik can remember no other dominion but that of the Ouroussi, which has thereby acquired the stamp of eternal fitness, and become stereotyped in the fatalist's creed. Samarkand may be looked upon as absolutely Russian, if not in part European; more Russian certainly than Benares is English, and far more European than is Peshawur.

A rumour is from time to time circulated in the European newspapers that the Amir of Bokhara is about to apply to Russia for the reddition of Samarkand; and it has even been stated that this was the object of a complimentary embassy recently (March 1889) sent by Seid Abdul Ahad to the Czar. It is true that years ago, before the Russian position in Central Asia was as stable as it has since become, and when the apprehensions of Europe required to be calmed, declarations were made by Russia of her intention to restore the city to its native rulers; and as late as 1870 Prince Gortchakoff assured Sir Andrew Buchanan, the British Ambassador at St. Petersburg, that "it was the desire of the Emperor to restore Samarkand to Bokhara; but that there was some difficulty in ascertaining how this could be done without a loss of dignity and without obtaining guarantees for the welfare of the population which had accepted the sovereignty of Russia." It is unnecessary to say that there never was the slightest intention of carrying out such an engagement, which if a Russian diplomat alone could have given, an English diplomat also would alone have believed. Still less is there any likelihood of such an absurdity now. Its revival is one of the colossal mare's nests discovered by the Russian Press.

At the end of the street in which stands the humble lodgment that presumed at the period of my visit to call itself a *Gastinitsa*, or hotel, loom up against the sky the gigantic walls and leaning towers of the three big *medresses* facing upon the Righistan, or public square, of the city of Tamerlane. The two cities, ancient and modern, are, however, separated by a bare stony hill, once occupied by the fortress and palace of the sovereign. Its walls have now been almost entirely demolished; and in their place are to be seen the trim outline and modern fortifications of the Russian citadel. Within this building, which is entered by a drawbridge across a moat, is still preserved part of the Amir's former palace; and here at the end of a court surrounded by an open colonnade is to be seen, behind an iron railing, the *Koktash*, or coronation-stone, of the Timurid sovereigns, the Central Asian equivalent to the Westminster slab from Scone. This celebrated object has been elaborately described by Schuyler and Lansdell. It is a mistake, however, to suppose that it always or has long reposed here. Timur's palace was some distance away to the west; and the *Koktash* was shifted to the citadel by one of the later Bokharan Amirs in this century.

In another part of the citadel was the Zindan, or prison, where, at the time of the Russian occupation, a subterranean dungeon existed like those to which allusion has been made at Bokhara and Karshi. Prisoners were let down into it by ropes; and the grooves which these had worn were visible in the stone lining of the top. How universal a method of

The cupola that overhangs the last resting-place of the great conqueror himself.

punishment this has always been throughout the East may be illustrated both by the parallel of Jerusalem in the seventh century B.C., when Jeremiah "was let down with cords into the dungeon of Malchiah that was in the court of the prison; and in the dungeon there was no water, but mire; so Jeremiah sunk in the mire"; and by that of Cairo under the Mamluks, where a similar pit, filled with vermin, and emitting noisome odours, was filled up in 1329 A.D.

Beyond the citadel, and on the other side of a slight valley, the native or ancient Samarkand covers the slope of a broad elevation, and from a dusty wilderness of flat roofs lifts up the glories of its mighty college gateways, its glazed and glittering arches, its leaning minarets, and its ribbed and enamelled domes. On the right hand, above a garden of fruit-trees, emerges the cupola that overhangs the last resting-place of the great conqueror himself. In the centre of the landscape are the three huge medresses or universities that frame the noblest public square in the world. On the left are the portentous ruins of the medresse and mosque of

The Gur Amir, or Tomb of Tamerlane, the most interesting ruin of Samarkand, where in 1405 the body of the conqueror, embalmed with musk and rose-water, and wrapped in linen, was laid in an ebony coffin.

Bibi Khanym, the Chinese wife of Timur, and at a little greater distance is the exquisite cluster of mosques and mausoleums, raised in honour of a saint whose immortality is expressed by the title of Shah Zindeh, or the Living King. A few words may be permitted about each of these.

The Gur Amir, or Tomb of Tamerlane, is both from the historic and the romantic point of view the most interesting ruin of Samarkand. Here in 1405 the body of the conqueror, embalmed with musk and rose-water, and wrapped in linen, was laid in an ebony coffin, and deposited beneath the engraved tombstone that we still behold in the vault. The interest of travellers seems usually to have been concentrated upon the upper chamber of the mausoleum, where, after the Eastern fashion, a series of cenotaphs, corresponding to the actual sepulchres below, are disposed upon the floor. The most noteworthy of these, covered with a block of greenish-black stone, said to be nephrite or jade, is that of Timur. The slab has evidently at some time been wrenched from its place and broken in twain; though it is not certain whether the fracture is to be attributed, as the legend runs, to an attempted violation by Nadir Shah. Around the walls of the tomb chamber is a wainscoting of hexagonal slabs of stone, variously described by travellers as agate, jasper, and gypsum. The last designation is nearest the mark; for they are of that species of alabaster, somewhat transparent in texture, but with an under colour like the sea waves, that is frequently met with in Oriental countries, and is familiar to visitors in Algeria and Egypt. The original tiles and decorations have been stripped or have fallen from the upper part of the walls; and, speaking generally, the entire fabric, which is in a sadly dilapidated and ruined condition, is disappointing to those who approach it with artistic expectations, and cannot be compared with the majestic sepulchres of the later Moguls in India, such as the mausoleum of Akbar the Great at

Sikundra. Nevertheless, the place has a certain attraction not perhaps unconnected with its lamentable decay. Though I do not pretend to understand the impulse that drives pilgrims in shoals to the graves of the departed great, yet there is something inspiring, even if it be a melancholy inspiration, in standing above the dust of one who was both a king among statesmen and a statesman among kings, whose deeds even at this distance of time alike astonish and appal, and whose monumental handiwork, still surviving around, a later and more civilised age has never attempted to equal, and has barely availed to rescue from utter ruin.

We next pass to the Righistan, or centre of the town, and to its triple glory of *medresses*, or religious colleges, those of Ulug Beg, the grandson of Timur (1421), of Shir Dar, or the Lion-bearing (1601) – so called from its bearing in enamelled tiles on its *façade* the Persian lion – and of Tillah Kari, or the Goldcovered (1618) – so named because of the gilding that once adorned its face. I have hazarded the statement that the Righistan of Samarkand was originally, and is still even in its ruin, the noblest public square in the world. I know of nothing in the East approaching it in massive simplicity and grandeur; and nothing in Europe, save perhaps on a humbler scale – the Piazza di San Marco at Venice – which can even aspire to enter the competition. No European spectacle indeed can adequately be compared with it, in our inability to point to an open space in any Western city that is commanded on three of its four sides by Gothic cathedrals of the finest order. For it is clear that the *medresse* of Central Asian Mahometanism is both in its architectural scope and design a lineal counterpart and forerunner of the minster of the West. Instead of the intricate sculpture and tracery crowning the pointed archways of the Gothic front, we see the enamelled tiles of Persia, framing a portal of stupendous magnitude. For the flanking minster towers or spires are substituted two soaring minarets. The central lantern of the West is anticipated by the Saracenic dome, and in lieu of artificial colour thrown through tinted panes, from the open heavens shine down the azure of the Eastern sky and the glory of the Eastern sun. What Samarkand must have been in its prime when these great fabrics emerged from the mason's hands, intact, and glittering with all the effulgence of the rainbow, their chambers crowded with students, their sanctuaries thronged by pilgrims, and their corporations endowed by kings, the imagination can still make some endeavour to depict.

Upon the structural features I shall confine myself to three observations. The minarets of all the *medresses* appear to be slightly out of the perpendicular, those of the college of Ulug Beg, which, as has been seen, is 200 years older than its fellows, conspicuously so. In a locality which has frequently been shaken by earthquakes, it surely needs no exceptional gifts either of acuteness or credulity to attribute to natural causes an irregularity so extravagant that no Oriental architect, whatever his taste for the unsymmetrical or bizarre, could ever have perpetrated it. And yet we find competent writers exhausting their inventiveness in far-fetched interpretations. Schuyler says the inclination is an optical illusion. Mme. Ujfalvy attributes it to the skill of the builders. M. Moser also speaks of it

as an architectural *tour de force*. Krestovski suggests a religious meaning. But Dr. Lansdell emerges triumphant from the competition of perverse ingenuity; for, having ascended one of the minarets himself, he proclaims the original discovery that there is no inclination at all!

Nowhere is the influence of country, of climate, and of natural resources upon architecture more noticeable than in the buildings of Samarkand. While the mildness and dryness of the atmosphere enabled the architect to dispense with many essentials of our Northern styles, on the other hand the poverty of local resources compelled him to go far afield for his decoration, and to be content with brick as his staple material. Persian artificers seem to have been almost exclusively employed upon the structures of Samarkand; and the wonderful enamelled tiles by which they were embellished had in all probability been burnt and glazed in Persian ovens. What Eastern architects were accomplishing at the same time with richer means at their disposal, may be seen in the mosques and mausoleums of the Mahometan conquerors of Hindostan. Timur, it is true, was antecedent by a century and a half to his descendants Humayun and Akbar, whose glorious erections we see at Agra and Delhi. But the Shir Dar and Tillah Kari *medresses* were almost exactly synchronous with the fabrics of Jehangir and Shah Jehan, with the Agran tomb of Itmad-ud-Dowlah, with the Pearl Mosque, loveliest of private chapels, in the citadel at Delhi, and with that most perfect of tributes ever raised to a lost love, the Taj Mahal on the banks of the Jumna. There, in

The Medresse *of Ulug Beg, the grandson of Timur.*

177

the southern clime, amid the abundant wealth and resources of Hindostan, the architect's waste was not satisfied with anything short of marble
and precious stones. Artists must even be imported from Europe; and the
luxuriant elegance of Florentine detail is wedded to the august symmetry
of Saracenic forms.

Nevertheless it is in the magnificent simplicity and solemn proportion
of the latter that the edifices of Samarkand remain without a rival.
Differing circumstances in the different countries overrun by the Arabs –
the influence of previous styles, local and climatic conditions, the genius
of individual masters, or the traditions of particular schools – produced a
wide variety of types, from the royal palace of Delhi to that of Granada,
from the shrines of Shiraz and Meshed to the chapels of Palermo, from
the mosques of Damascus and Cairo to those of Cordova and Kairwhan.
In some places majestic outline, in others intricate detail, was the object
or the achievement of the artist. Fancy was here subordinated to funda-
mental canons, was there allowed to run riot in complicate involution.
But it cannot be doubted that the true and essential character of the
Saracenic style is expressed in grandeur rather than in delicacy, in
chastity rather than in ornament. It was by the grouping of great masses,
and by the artistic treatment of simple lines, that the Arab architects first
impressed their genius upon the world; and in this respect no more
stately product of their talent can anywhere be found than in the half-
fallen monuments of the city of Tamerlane.

The remaining ruins I must dismiss briefly. The most imposing remains at Samarkand, in bulk and dimensions, are undeniably the
medresse and mosque of Bibi Khanym, the Chinese consort of Timur,
whom the courtly Don Ruy designated as "Caño; the chief wife of the
Great Lord". They are said to have been erected respectively by the royal
lady and her illustrious spouse; and it was this mosque that Timur caused
to be pulled down as soon as it was finished, because the entrance was too
low, and whose rebuilding he superintended with imperious energy from
a litter. What these buildings once were we can only faintly realise by the
aid of the colossal piles of masonry that still stand, and that tower above
the other ruins of Samarkand as high as do the vaulted arches of Con-
stantine's Basilica over the southern end of the Forum at Rome. The only
perfect relic in the ruined enclosure is the vast *rahle*, or lectern, which
stands on nine low columns in the centre and which once bore in its
V-shaped cleft a ponderous Koran. This has survived, because it is of
marble instead of brick, and therefore was too heavy for any conqueror to
transport, and too solid for any vandal to destroy. The remaining parts of
the building are slowly and steadily falling to ruin; and in time, unless
steps are taken to arrest the process, will become a shapeless heap of
bricks.

The cluster of mosques and chapels with seven small cupolas, that bear
the name of the Living King – its eponymous saint having been a near
relative of the Prophet, who was martyred here in early times, and who is
supposed to be lurking with his decapitated head in his hand at the
bottom of a well, although with curious inconsistency his coffined body is

The medresse and mosque of Bibi Khanym, the Chinese consort of Timur, which Timur caused to be pulled down as soon as it was finished because the entrance was too low.

also an object of worship in the same building – is both the most perfect and the most graceful of the ruins of Samarkand. A ruin unfortunately it is; for domes have collapsed, inscriptions have been defaced, and the most exquisite enamelling has perished. But still, as we mount the thirty-seven steps that lead upwards between narrow walls, at intervals in the masonry there open out small recessed mosques and tomb chambers with faultless honeycomb groining, executed in moulded and coloured tiles. Gladly would I expatiate upon the beauty of these Samarkandian tiles – turquoise and sapphire and green and plum-coloured and orange, crusted over with a rich siliceous glaze, and inscribed with mighty Kufic letters – by which these glorious structures were once wholly and are still in part adorned.

But it is more relevant to point out that beyond having patched up the most glaring traces of dilapidation and made a few attempts, with deplorable results, to replace destroyed ornament, the Russians have done nothing, and are doing nothing, whatever to preserve these sacred relics either from wanton demolition or from natural decay; and that, what with the depredations of vandals, the shock of earthquakes, and the lapse of time, the visitor in the twentieth century may find cause to enquire with resentful surprise what has become of the fabled grandeurs of the old Samarkand. A Society for the Preservation of Ancient Monuments should at once be formed in Russian Central Asia, and a custodian should be appointed to each of the more important ruins. But this is a step which can hardly be expected from a Government which has never, outside of Russia, shown the faintest interest in antiquarian preservation or research, and which would sit still till the crack of doom upon a site that was known to contain the great bronze Athene of Pheidias, or the lost works of Livy. While visiting the Shah Zindeh, I was the fortunate witness of one of those rare sunsets that are sometimes visible in the East, and which, though they cannot compete with the troubled grandeur of our Western skies, are yet incomparable in their tranquil glory.

The northern outside wall of Shah Zindeh is bordered by a Mussulman necropolis, which is as lugubrious and desolate-looking a spot as cemeteries in Mahometan countries usually are. Broken pillars, displaced tombstones, and desecrated brick vaults litter the drab and dusty surface. As we stood in one of the elevated courts overlooking the boundary-wall, we observed a funeral proceeding on the other side. The corpse was brought up lying loosely on a kind of open bier which resembled a sofa, and was presently tumbled without much ceremony into a ditch which had been prepared in the sandy soil. There was a large attendance of mourners, all males, who appeared to take an inquisitive interest in the proceedings, but there was no show of grief or attempt at a service. Climbing still higher up the stairway, we emerged on the hill behind the tomb-chamber of the saint. The sun was just sinking: and it was one of those superb evenings only known in the East, when for a few seconds, amid a hush as of death, we seem to realise

The light that never was on sea or land:

and then in a moment the twilight rushes down with violet wings, and all nature swoons in her embrace. In the short space of preternatural luminousness that preceded, the broken edge of the Penjakent mountains cut the sky like blue steel and seemed to sever the Zerafshan valley from the outer world. Inside the magic circle described by their lofty shapes a splendid belt of trees plunged momentarily into a deeper and more solemn green, contrasting vividly with the purple of the mountain background. The middle space was filled by the colossal arches and riven domes of Bibi Khanyin, which loomed up above the native city in all the majesty and pathos of irretrievable ruin. Below and all around, a waste of grey sandhills was encumbered with half-fallen tombstones and mouldering graves. Here and there a horsehair plume, floating from the end of a rickety pole, betrayed the last resting-place of a forgotten sheikh or saint. The only evidence of life was supplied by the horses of the mourners, themselves out of sight at the moment, which were picketed amid the waste of graves. Presently round the corner of the mosque emerged the long line of turbaned Orientals, grave and silent. Each mounted his beast without speaking a word and rode away. At that instant a band of turquoise blue seemed to encircle the horizon and to flush upwards towards the zenith, where light amber skeins hung entangled like the filaments of a golden veil. As these drifted apart and lost the transient glory; as the turquoise deepened into sapphire and died down into dusk; as first the belt of trees and then the outer belt of mountains was wiped out, a long cry trembled through the breathless void. It was the voice of the muezzin from a neighbouring minaret, summoning the faithful to evening prayer.

A Society for the Preservation of Ancient Monuments should at once be formed in Russian Central Asia.

I was told on high authority at Samarkand that the Russian garrison consisted entirely of Cossack regiments, and amounted to a total of 10,000 men. I doubted this statement from the first, because of the absence of any sign of such large numbers and the lack of motive for keeping so powerful a force at such a place; and my suspicions were subsequently justified by the discovery that there was only half that total of men, including but one Cossack regiment and three batteries of artillery. Here, as elsewhere, I found it excessively difficult to reconcile the conflicting utterances of my different informants, each of whom might have imparted correct information if he had been able or willing to do so. I say "able" because I ended by forming the opinion that one of the commonest features of Russian character is a constitutional incapacity for exactitude of statement.

The population of Samarkand is estimated at about 40,000 persons, of whom the Europeans number 6,000, while there are as many as 1,500 Jews. The bazaars struck me as greatly inferior in every way to those of Bokhara, and there was a marked contrast in many respects between the native life of the two cities, the one still independent, the other Russian for twenty years. In Samarkand the urban population, or Sarts, as they are here called, were much more humbly and shabbily dressed; there was no evidence of wealth or dignity or leisure, and the street sights were generally squalid and uninteresting. Even the native bazaar has been thoroughly transformed under Russian rule, large blocks of crooked alleys having been swept away to make place for broad boulevards converging from the different points of the compass upon the Righistan. In driving the latter in straight lines through the heart of the city, the Russians have been unconsciously following an example set them nearly 500 years ago by their great forerunner Tamerlane; for again we owe to the agreeable gossip of the Spanish Ambassador of King Henry III of Castile the knowledge that "The lord (*i.e.* Timur) ordered a street to be made through the city, pulling down all houses that stood in the line, a street very broad and covered with a vaulted roof, and windows to let in the light from one end of the city to the other."

Samarkand has, as I have indicated, more than once been made the residence of important political refugees, whom it was to the interest of Russia to conciliate, to watch, or to entertain. Abdurrahman Khan, the present Amir of Afghanistan, was here for many years, and during his residence married a slave girl from Wakhan, who had already become the mother of his two eldest surviving sons. His cousin Is-hak, the recent pretender, who had fled with him upon the triumph of Shir Ali, shared his exile at Samarkand, and returned in his company in 1880, receiving as the reward of his assumed fidelity the governorship of Afghan Turkestan. Both of them are said to have left Samarkand with a less favourable opinion of their hosts than that with which they came, and to have roundly abused the Russians afterwards; though the attitude of Is-hak may be presumed once more to have changed, now that he is again dependent upon their hospitality, and possibly expects in the future to be indebted to them for a throne. I could not discover that at the time of my

visit there were any of these interesting exiles in the city, though a rumour – denied as soon as uttered – of the return of Is-hak to his old quarters was already in circulation.

While at Samarkand the chance was presented to me of making under the best auspices a visit to Tashkent. Though the distance between the two places is considerable – 190 miles – and can only be covered by road, I eagerly grasped this opportunity of forming even a slight acquaintance with the capital of Russia in the East; being anxious to observe the visible effects of a dominion that has now lasted for over twenty years, to acquaint myself with the ideas that are rumoured to prevail in its military circles, and to contrast its Court life and etiquette with the analogous British *régime* at Calcutta. I also wished to form some opinion as to the feasibility of an extension of the Transcaspian line from the Zerafshan province into Turkestan.

It was not till I was well on my way to Tashkent that I realised how great, from the most selfish and personal point of view, the advantages of that railway had been. The luckless traveller condemned to the amenities of a tarantass across the Golodnaya, or Famished Steppe, hankers after the second-class carriages of General Annenkoff as eagerly as did the Israelites in similar surroundings after the flesh-pots of Egypt. I know that it is the fashion of English writers to decry, just as it is of Russians to extol, the tarantass; but I must confess in this case to a full and honest share in the prejudices of my countrymen. A kind of ramshackle wooden boat, resting on long wooden poles, which themselves repose on the

Even the native bazaar has been thoroughly transformed under Russian rule.

wooden axles of wooden wheels – this is the sorrowful and springless vehicle in which two of us were to travel 380 miles, and in which travellers have often covered thousands. There is one advantage in the fabrics being entirely of wood – namely, that if it breaks down *en route*, as sooner or later it is perfectly certain to do, its repair can be effected without much difficulty. Too nicely pieced a structure would indeed be unsuited to the conditions of Central Asian travel; for the vehicle is required to ford rivers and cross deserts, now buried in mud, now plunging heavily through sand, to resist concussions, and to emerge from mishaps that would dislocate any finer piece of workmanship. The Russians have reduced to a science the subjugation of the tarantass by means of straw and mattresses; but the less skilful Englishman, in the rough places where there is no road, is tossed about like a cork on tumbled water. Fortunately, the remaining difficulties usually associated with such a method of locomotion are here somewhat curtailed; for there is a postal service along the road between Samarkand and Tashkent, with relays of post-horses at the various stations, placed at distances of about fifteen miles apart. A *Podorojna*, or special order, must first be procured from the authorities. This entitles the traveller to a change of horses at each station; though, even so, he is far from safe, for the intimation that all the available horses are tired or unfed or still feeding, which occurs from time to time with mathematical regularity, may compel him either to wait half a day in a grim post-house in the middle of an odious desert, or to hire whatever animals he can procure from any well-disposed rustic possessing a stable in the neighbourhood. The horses are harnessed to the tarantass in a *troika* – *i.e.* three abreast; the middle horse between the shafts having its neck held tightly up by a bearing-rein attached to a high wooden arch rising above its head, while the outside horses are not even confined within traces, but gallop along in random fashion, with their heads, as a rule, looking inquisitively round the corner. A different driver, Tajik, or Uzbeg, or Kirghiz, each with unmistakable physiognomy, mounts the box at each post-house, and at the end of his stage absorbs without either gratitude or protest a modest gratuity.

The road to Tashkent is roughly divided into three sections by the mountain defile known as the Gates of Tamerlane and the main stream of the Syr Daria or Jaxartes; and the distances between its principal points are as follows:

Samarkand to Jizak . . . 65 miles
Jizak to Tchinaz . . . 83 miles
Tchinaz to Tashkent . . . 42 miles

Our outward journey occupied thirty hours, including halts at the post-stations; the return journey, upon which we suffered from scarcity of horses, thirty-six. Russian officers, travelling at the maximum rate of speed, have covered it in twenty-four and even in twenty-two hours.

Leaving Samarkand on the north-east, we skirt the hill Tchupan-Ata – once crowned by the great observatory of Ulug Beg, but now by the white-washed tomb of a local saint – and pass at no great distance from the mass of crumbling *tumuli* and mounds that mark the site of an ancient city, associated with the legendary hero Afrasiab, and supposed to have been the predecessor of the Maracanda of the Greeks. Heaps of rubbish and the accumulations of centuries cover an immense extent, not unlike the ruins of Fostat or Old Cairo. Excavations have been pursued in a half-hearted and disjointed fashion by the Russians, but no deliberate or scientific effort has been made to explore whatever secrets of the past – and they must be manifold and important – the ruins of Kaleh-i-Afrasiab can tell. This is one of the many chances of the future.

After traversing a succession of gardens and orchards, we come at the distance of a few miles from Samarkand to the fords of the main stream of the Zerafshan. It courses swiftly along over a very stony bed, and was divided at this season of the year into four or five channels, of which none were over a foot and a half in depth. The space between its banks is, however, several hundred yards in width; and in summer, when the snows in the mountains melt, is for a short time filled by a raging torrent. Hard by are the ruins of two stupendous arches, meeting at an obtuse angle, which are called Shadman-Melik by the natives, and which tower magnificently above the attenuated volume of the autumnal stream. Nothing is known of the authorship or date of these huge remains; but it is conjectured that, placed as they are close to the spot where the Zerafshan divides into two main streams – the Ak Daria or White River, and the Kara Daria or Black River – they originally bridged the two channels at the angle of bifurcation. Near the Zerafshan in this quarter are several hundreds of acres that have been planted as a nursery garden by the Russians, and where are grown vines (of which there are no less than sixteen varieties in the country), acacias, and ilanthus.

Upon the other side of the river vegetation dwindles and finally disappears, and for many miles we proceed between the low hills of the Pass of Jilanuti, culminating at the northern end in a rocky portal where many a bloody conflict has been waged for the possession of the Zerafshan valley. The boastful record of two ancient conquerors is deeply incised on the smoothed face of the rock – of Ulug Beg, victorious in 1425, and of Abdullah Khan of Bokhara, Anthony Jenkinson's host, in 1571, when the inscription records that he slew 400,000 of the enemy, so that blood ran for a month in the river of Jizak. Very like in character, and not unlike, though less rugged in surroundings, are these sculptured trophies to the celebrated inscription of Trajan above the Iron Gates of the Danube in Europe. In spite of the deeds and names it commemorates, the Central Asian defile, in characteristic deference to the overpowering prestige of a single name, is known as the Gates of Tamerlane.

Not many miles beyond is the extensive but straggling town of Jizak, with a population of 4,000, the mouldering walls of whose former citadel serve as a forlorn reminder of the Russian victory of 1866. Then ensues the Waste of Hunger, very properly so called, for a more starved and sorry-looking region it would be difficult to conceive; and as the tarantass goes bumping along, with the bells hung in the high wooden arch over

185

the central horse's head jingling a wild discord, and the dust rolling up in suffocating volumes, the traveller too is very hungry for the end to arrive. He can draw but little repose or consolation from his halts at the post-houses, where a bare waiting-room with wooden tables and uncovered settees is placed at his disposal, and whose culinary resources do not rise above the meagre level of a cup of tea and a boiled egg. Any other or more extravagant rations he must bring with him.

At length we reach the Syr Daria, or Jaxartes, the second great river of Central Asia, terminating at present, like its greater brother the Oxus, in the Aral Sea. The channel here appeared to be over a quarter of a mile wide, and flowed along with a very rapid ochreous current. Our vehicle was driven bodily on to a big ferry boat, worked by the stream, and attached to a chain, the ferry being commanded by a fort on the northern bank. Here is the Russian town of Tchinaz, at a distance of three miles from the old native Tchinaz, which was taken in 1865. Then ensues another spell of dusty rutworn desert; and our vehicle selects this opportune moment to discard one of its wheels. But patience is at length rewarded, tall snow-capped mountains, which mean water, which in its turn means verdure, rise into view; we enter the valley of the Tchirtchik and its affluents, twenty-five miles in width; and amid the sound of running water, and under the shade of broad avenues of trees, forty miles after leaving the Syr Daria we approach the suburbs of the capital of Turkestan.

By the suburbs of Tashkent I need not refer to the environs only; for in reality the Russian town is one vast suburb, in which the houses stand apart amid trees and gardens interspersed with open spaces. The meaning of the name is "city of stone", a *lucus a non lucendo* title as far as either the Russian, or the native town, is concerned, though whether it applies more strictly to the ruins of old Tashkent, twenty miles away, I cannot say. The size and height of the trees, principally poplar, acacia, and willow, with which the streets of the new town are planted in double and even in quadruple rows, and which are of course only twenty years old, give a fair indication of what irrigation and this superb climate when in partnership can do. A shoot has simply to be stuck into the ground, and the rest may safely be left to nature.

Tashkent is a very large city, for it covers an area as extensive as Paris, though with a population, not of 2,500,000, but of 120,000, of which 100,000 are congregated in the native or Sart quarter. The Russian civil and military population are computed at the same figure, 10,000 each, and so large are the enclosures or gardens in which the houses stand apart that the majority of the residents would seem to have attained the ideal of Arcadian bliss expressed elsewhere in the historical phrase, "Three acres and a cow". A valley bisects the two portions of the town, native and European, which are as separate in every particular as are the lives of the double element in the population, neither interfering nor appearing to hold communication with the other. In the capitals of India, at Bombay, Calcutta, and Madras, there is far greater fusion, both in private and in public life – the Parsees at Bombay, the resident princes and noblemen at

Calcutta, and the most influential native merchants in all three, mingling habitually in Anglo-Indian society, and taking a prominent part, in some cases in government, in others in the management of public institutions. In Tashkent, on the other hand, several obstacles preclude a similar amalgamation – the purely military character of the administration, the dearth of any wealthy or capable men among the natives, and the recency of the Russian conquest. I remember once reading the remark that "In Russia the discipline of the camp is substituted for the order of the city; martial law is the normal condition of life"; and of no Russian city that I have seen did this strike me as more true than of Tashkent. Uniforms are everywhere, parade grounds and barracks abound, the extensive *entourage* associated with a great administrative centre is military and not civil in character. It is hardly surprising that under such a system practical or far-seeing projects for commercial and industrial development should not be forthcoming; that the fiscal balance should be habitually on the wrong side of the budget; or that Chauvinistic and aggressive ideas should prevail. Where the ruling class is entirely military, and where promotion is slow, it would be strange if war, the sole available avenue to distinction, were not popular.

Tashkent is, perhaps, less than it used to be, the refuge of damaged reputations and shattered fortunes, whose only hope of recovery lay in the chances afforded on the battlefield. But it is still the compulsory place of exile to which the young spend-thrift and the veteran offender are

The Russian population have attained the ideal of Arcadian bliss.

187

Tashkent is, perhaps less than it used to be, the refuge of damaged reputations.

equally consigned, the official purgatory following upon the Emperor's displeasure. One of the principal houses is inhabited by a Grand Duke, a first cousin of the Czar, who is said to be a very *mauvais sujet*. He married the daughter of a police-officer at Orenburg, and is reported to drink and to beat his wife. The exile of this degenerate scion of royalty is understood to be lifelong.

I have already, in an earlier chapter, spoken of the rumours that had prevailed in the military circles of Tashkent, shortly before my visit, of an impending invasion of Afghanistan. It is therefore with pleasure that I record the fact that the present Governor-General (General Rosenbach), whose hospitality I was fortunate enough to enjoy, bears a very different reputation – having, it is said, been appointed by the present Emperor to create a diversion from the adventurous policy of his predecessors, Kaufmann and Tchernaieff, and in order to develop more carefully the moral and material resources of the country. If I may judge from the general's own words, it is in the latter object that he has himself been principally interested. For he spoke to me of the enormous growth in the produce of cotton, the export of which from Tashkent has multiplied twenty-five-fold in the last five years; and when, mindful of the old charge that the Russians have done nothing to improve the mental and moral condition of the subject population, I enquired whether any steps had been taken to open schools for the natives, he informed me that four

The old charge is that the Russians have done nothing to improve the mental and moral condition of the subject population.

such schools had been started in Tashkent, with an attendance of from thirty to forty at each, though at present the natives exhibit no great desire to learn, and that similar institutions had been started in Khokand, Hodjent, Katta Kurgan, and Samarkand. He also told me that an infirmary had been opened for native women in the capital, and was largely resorted to by them. Differing from Mr. Schuyler, who wrote that "Tashkent is not a manufacturing nor an agricultural centre, nor is it a trade centre," he regarded his capital as the natural and physical nucleus of Central Asian trade, and did not anticipate that its supremacy would be endangered by the greater advantages now enjoyed by Samarkand. General Rosenbach has now been for four years in Turkestan; and while I was there was said to be likely to leave for some less onerous post in Russia. I fancy, however, that his own inclinations would, and I am confident that public interests should, induce him to devote a somewhat longer time to the further development of this still backward country.

Benefiting by the hospitality of Government House, I had some opportunity of observing the style in which the Yarim Padishah, or Half-King, as he is described in Central Asia, represents the Imperial Government. Schuyler, in his book and in the report which he penned for the American Government, drew a vivid picture of the state kept up by

The Military Club at Tashkent, a city where uniforms are everywhere, parade grounds and barracks abound.

Kaufmann, who never went out without an escort of 100 mounted Cossacks, who permitted no one to sit down in his presence, and whose return to Tashkent was always signalised by triumphal arches and the firing of cannon. General Rosenbach has very different ideas; and the Government House *ménage* is now pushed to the extreme of simplicity – an example which, while its effect upon the native population is immaterial, there being no class of sufficient importance to be dazzled by a show, is unquestionably of great service to the Russian military circles, in which the most reckless extravagance used formerly to prevail. Madame de Ujfalvy-Bourdon in her book spoke of Government House as "a veritable palace, with a truly splendid interior, which could not be surpassed in any capital in Europe"; but I fancy that her faculty of perspective must have been temporarily disorganised by the prior experiences of a tarantass and the Kirghiz Steppes. As a matter of fact, its furniture and appointments are almost jejune in their modesty. The only two large rooms, the ball-room and the dining-room, are practically unfurnished. There is no throne-room or dais; and the only emblems of royalty are the oil-paintings of the late Czar and his wife, and of the present Emperor and Empress, which hang upon the walls. The general is very proud of an ante-chamber or smoking-room, the panels and coffered cornices of which have been entirely carved and painted in Oriental style by Sart workmen, and upholstered with divans of parti-coloured Bokharan velvet. When he drives out, his landau is drawn by a troika or three handsomely caparisoned horses, whilst the livery affected by his Tartar coachman is a black velvet cap with peacock feathers stuck in the brim. I cannot imagine a greater contrast to the state observed by the Indian Viceroy, who in a country famed for its lavish ostentation, its princely wealth, and its titled classes, is obliged to support the style of a sovereign, who resides in a palace, the corridors of which are crowded with gorgeous figures in scarlet and gold liveries, who drives out accompanied by a brilliant escort, and whose levées are as rigid in their etiquette as those of Buckingham Palace or St. James'.

A valley bisects the two portions of the town, native and European neither interfering nor appearing to hold communication with the other.

Curzon of Kedleston

RUSSIAN CENTRAL ASIA
and the
TRANSCASPIAN RAILWAY

Natural Scale 1 : 5,900,000

40 20 30 40 50   100   150 English Miles

0 10 20 30 40 50   100   150 Russian Versts

..ts, o Wells, :.Ruins, ⚒ Mines, ✕ Passes ━━━ Bridges
Heights in English Feet.

EXPLANATION
of geographical terms belonging to oriental languages.
Persian
Ab =Water ; Rud =River ; Pul =Bridge ; Koh =Mountains ; Kala =castle ; Sufeid =whi..
Turkish
Su =Water ; Chai =River ; Kuyu =Well ; Dagh =Mount ; Tepe =summit, top, hill ;
Dere =valley ; Tekke =Mahomedan monastery ; ak =white ; kara =black ; kizil =..